Leading Young People to Mary

For Parents, Teachers, and Others

Leading Young People to Mary

For Parents, Teachers, and Others

Mary Kathleen Glavich, SND

Cover art by Sandro Bottticelli from "Madonna of the Book"

Imprint: Independently published

ISBN-10: **9798815949898**

Dedicated to Mary,
our Blessed Mother and Queen of Heaven,
who watches over us and prays for us
with loving concern

Introduction

The cover of the December 2015 *National Geographic* bore the same art as the cover of this book: Sandro Botticelli's delicate face of our Blessed Mother from his painting "Madonna of the Book." Superimposed on it were the words "Mary, the Most Powerful Woman in the World." Inside the magazine was a lengthy feature article about Jesus' mother.

More art, more literature, and more music are about Mary than any other woman. Why is so much attention paid to this first-century woman? She deserves it. As someone pithily put it: No Mary, no Jesus. And as a wit paraphrased that saying: "Know Mary, Know Jesus." (Interestingly, Jesus bore a striking resemblance to Mary because all his DNA came from her.)

Out of all the women who ever lived or will live on our planet, God chose Mary of Nazareth to be his mother. As a young Jewish teenager, she agreed to God's amazing and daunting proposal. Surrendering her body and her whole life, she brought Jesus, the Son of God, into the world. She taught the God-man what it meant to be a human being: how to walk, talk, and eat, among other things. By wholeheartedly cooperating with God's plan from Jesus' conception to his crucifixion, Mary participated in the salvation of humankind.

This holy woman is also our devoted mother, whom Jesus bequeathed to us on Calvary. When we honor her, we honor and please her Son. Mary is our protector and most powerful intercessor in heaven. In loving concern for us, she places our requests before almighty God. It makes sense that we learn as much as we can about our Blessed Mother and take steps to acquaint others with her.

Leading Young People to Mary is a collection of interesting, enjoyable activities that will help students of all ages expand their knowledge of their heavenly mother. This knowledge will lead them to love and honor her and consequently draw them closer to God, who loves her immensely. The activities range in difficulty from simple ones for preschoolers to challenging ones for teens and beyond. From this smorgasbord choose those that are age-appropriate or adapt others to your situation. Anyone who is interested in learning more about Mary is bound to benefit from the information and activities in this book.

As a Sister of Notre Dame (Our Lady), who has taught every grade from first to twelfth, I found it a joy to write this Marian book. My hope is that many teachers, parents, grandparents, and godparents will find it a helpful resource not only for teaching about our Blessed Mother but learning more about her themselves.

Mary Kathleen Glavich, SND

October 7, 2021

Feast of Our Lady of the Rosary

Contents

Appendix

Chapter 1

Saint Mary of Nazareth

The Marianum in Rome, a pontifical institute for the study of Mariology (the theology of Mary), offers a master's degree and a doctorate in the field. Its library holds more than 85,000 books on Mary! How did we come to know anything about this woman who lived in an obscure village some two thousand years ago? Our primary and almost sole source of information about Saint Mary is Sacred Scripture, God's Word. All four Gospels speak of her. They recount only a few events in Mary's life, but these events are significant. Through them we come to know what agreeing to be the Mother of God entailed, Mary's sterling character, and her spirituality.

In addition, imaginative stories about Mary's birth, childhood, and marriage are found in the *Protoevangelium of James* (Gospel of James). Although this document dating back to 150 AD is apocryphal (not considered divinely inspired), from it the Church drew the traditional names for Mary's parents. One of its stories also gave rise to the November 21 celebration of the Presentation of Mary in the Temple at age three.

Mary's Life

Mary was a Jewish peasant who lived in the Asian country of Israel during late BC and early AD years. Historians studying literature from that period and archaeologists delving into ancient ground continually make discoveries that shed light on her life and circumstances. Some facts about Mary, however, will probably remain hidden. For example: What did she look like? When did her husband die? Was Mary's sister who stood near the cross a younger sister or a sister-in-law? (John 19:25). Did the resurrected Jesus appear to his mother on Easter? What was her life like after Pentecost?

1

Activities

• Research information about Mary and her life and prepare a written or an oral report. Work individually or in a group, dividing the topics. Here are possible questions to answer:

What did the historical Mary look like—her eyes, hair, skin tone, height?

Who were her parents?

What was her hometown and its population?

What was her country and who ruled it?

In what kind of house did she live?

What were her clothes like? Did she wear jewelry?

What did she eat? How was it prepared?

What were her household tasks?

What language did she speak?

To which Jewish tribe did she belong?

Who were her religious leaders?

What Jewish feasts did she celebrate?

What religious customs did she observe?

How did her society regard women?

Was Mary literate?

How did she pray?

How were marriages arranged?

About how old was Mary when she became God's mother?

Who was Mary's husband? What do we know about him?

• Give a PowerPoint show "A Day in the Life of Mary." Include answers to some questions above.

• Write an essay comparing Mary's life to yours.

• Learn about life in Nazareth by going to www.nazarethvillage.com and seetheholyland.net/Nazareth.

Mary's Name

Mary is our English name for the Mother of God. In her language it was probably Miriam or Maryam, the name of Moses' sister. In Latin this name is translated Maria. For centuries, girls and even boys have been named Mary or some form of it in honor of our Blessed Mother. In the musical *West Side Story,* Tony, who loves Maria, sings that her name is the most beautiful sound he ever heard. In the song he says "Maria" twenty-seven times! Likewise, the Church, who loves Mary, treasures her name and celebrates the Most Holy Name of Mary on September 12, four days after commemorating her birth.

Saint Louis de Montfort, an ardent fan of Mary, thought up this play on words: "God the Father gathered all the waters together and called them seas or *maria* [Latin for "seas"]. He gathered all his grace together and called it Mary or Maria."

Activities

• Find out the meaning of the name Mary.

• List names that are derived from the name Mary such as Marie. Then add other names that refer to Mary, such as Madonna (which means "my lady") and Dolores (which means "sorrows"). Include names taken from events related to her like Assumpta.

• Hold a contest to see who can compile the most Marian names.

• Think of people you know who are named Mary or a derivative of it.

• Discover religious communities of men and women that are named for Our Lady.

• Find the letters *M, A, R,* and *I* in this monogram for Maria (Mary). This symbol may appear with a cross or a crown above it or surrounded by twelve stars. Locate variations of this monogram on the Internet.

• Think of things and places that are named for our Blessed Mother. Here is a start: The flagship Christopher Columbus sailed on to America was the Santa Maria. Its full name was Saint Mary of the Immaculate Conception. Missionary and explorer Jacques Marquette, S.J., who discovered the Mississippi River, named it River of the Immaculate Conception. (Caution: Maryland was named by King Charles I of England for his wife, Queen Henrietta Maria.)

Mary's Holiness

Saint Mary is not a goddess but a flesh and blood woman who, however, by a special blessing of God, is full of grace. This means she shares in the divine life of the all-holy God. She is God's masterpiece, sinless and wholly pure from the first moment of her existence. In her case, the redemption that her Son brought about was retroactive. Because God chose Mary to be his Mother, he saw to it that her holiness exceeds that of all the Saints and angels. God made her Queen of Heaven.

Always cooperating with the Holy Spirit, Mary exemplifies every virtue and is an icon of the Beatitudes. As the first and best Christian, she is the ideal model for us. As our mother and intercessor, she assists us as we, too, try to be holy followers of her Son.

Activities

• List five of Mary's virtues. For each one provide an example of how she exhibited it.

• Discuss the virtue of Mary you most admire and why.

• Write a composition on one of the following topics. Draw a picture to accompany it.

Mary listened to God.
Mary trusted God.
Mary loved God.
Mary loved others.

- Mark off four columns on a sheet of paper and head them Listen, Trust, Love God, and Love Others. In the respective column list ways you could imitate your Blessed Mother by listening to God, trusting God, loving God, and loving others.

- Produce a skit in which someone your age displays a virtue of Our Lady.

- Find examples in the news of people who have acted or are acting like Mary.

- Explain how these metaphors for Mary are related to her holiness: waterfall, light, moon, tower, enclosed garden, God's Eden.

- Think of a woman you know who resembles Mary in that she shows one or more of Mary's beautiful qualities. Write an essay comparing the two women.

Mary's Ancestors

Tradition holds that Mary was a descendant of King David. Paul wrote that Jesus "was descended from David" (Romans 1:3). The Angel Gabriel told Mary that God would give to her Son "the throne of his ancestor David" (Luke 1:32). Joseph "was descended from the house and family of David" (Luke 2:4). It is not clear that Mary was descended from David. However, there are reasons to think so. As a descendant of David, Mary, like Joseph, would belong to the tribe of Judah, the leading tribe of the southern kingdom of Judah and the origin of the name Jews.

Jewish lineage in the Old Testament had been traced through fathers. Interestingly, history indicates that somewhere in the first century (about 10 AD to 70 AD) descent began to be traced through mothers.

Activities

- Draw Mary's family tree. Assume that she is descended from King David and begin with Abraham. After her name, add the name of her Son Jesus.

—

5

• Create a Jesse Tree, named for King David's father. It is decorated with symbols for people of the Old Testament.

    – Prepare a tree in one of these ways:

        Use a real or artificial evergreen tree.

        Stand a branch in a pail of cement, plaster of paris, soil, or rocks.

        Draw a tree on a large sheet of paper.

    – Prepare ornaments in one of these ways:

        Make the ornaments out of paper, dough, or other assorted materials, for example, toothpicks for Isaac's wood.

        Purchase readymade ornaments.

        Find printable sheets of ornaments to be colored and cut out.

        Locate templates that can be used to make ornaments from cloth.

Jesse Tree Ornaments

Adam and Eve *(apple)*

Noah *(ark, rainbow, dove with a branch)*

Abraham *(sword, altar)*

Isaac *(bundle of wood, ram in bush)*

Rebecca *(pitcher)*

Jacob *(ladder, well)*

Joseph *(coat of many colors)*

Moses *(burning bush, tablets of the Law)*

Levi *(lamb on an altar)*

Ruth *(sheaf of wheat)*

David *(crown, harp)*

Solomon *(temple)*

Judith *(sword)*

Isaiah *(scroll)*

Daniel *(lion)*

Esther *(six-pointed star and chain)*

John the Baptist *(shell)*

Saint Joseph *(carpenter's tools, staff)*

Mary *(lily, the letter* M*)*

Other symbols: City of Bethlehem, star, rising sun, key of David

On top of the tree, a chi-rho (for Christ):

Mary's Country

Christians call Israel the Holy Land because it is where Jesus and Mary lived; where our salvation was accomplished through the life, death, and resurrection of Christ; and where the Church was born. It is also the Promised Land that God gave to Abraham and his descendants. Christians, Jews, and Muslims consider that country sacred.

For those fortunate people who make a pilgrimage to Israel and visit its revered sites, the Gospels come to life. Reading them and hearing them proclaimed are never the same.

Activities

• Draw a map of Israel or create a clay or papier-mâché model. Include part of Egypt. Locate a map of first-century Israel on the Internet or in a book for a good example.

 – With large letters label Israel and Egypt.
 – With smaller letters label the three regions Galilee, Samaria, and Judea.
 – With the smallest letters label these features:

Nazareth	Jerusalem
Bethlehem	Sea of Galilee
Ain Karem	Jordan River
Cana	Dead Sea

• Find out what Israel's climate, weather, and terrain were like when Mary lived.

• Take a virtual tour of the Holy Land using one of the videos on youTube or by visiting www.holylandsite.com.

• Using a map of the Holy Land, determine approximately how many miles Mary traveled from the time of the Annunciation to the finding of Jesus in the Temple. Fittingly, one of her titles is Our Lady of the Highway. Here are journeys she made over a few years:

From Nazareth to Ain Karem to assist Elizabeth

From Nazareth to Bethlehem for the census

From Bethlehem to Jerusalem for the presentation of Jesus (Luke's Gospel)

From Bethlehem to Egypt to escape Herod (Matthew's Gospel)

From Egypt to Nazareth after Herod's death (Matthew's Gospel)

From Nazareth to Jerusalem for Passover

- View pictures of Marian sites in the Holy Land on the Internet or in a book. They may include the following:

Basilica of Saint Anne	Church at Cana
Basilica of the Annunciation	Chapel of Fright
Basilica of the Visitation	The Temple Mount
Basilica of the Nativity	Basilica of the Holy Sepulcher
Shepherd's Field	The Upper Room
Mary's Well	Church of the Dormition
Saint Joseph's Church	

- Draw a large map of Israel and on it indicate where the sites listed above are located.

- Write a report on one or more of the Marian sites in the Holy Land. Explain how they are associated with Our Lady.

- Invite someone who has been to the Holy Land to speak about the experience, especially visiting features related to Mary, such as the Basilica of the Annunciation in Nazareth and the Church of the Nativity in Bethlehem.

- Report on recent archaeological discoveries in the Holy Land pertaining to the Bible.

- Make a timeline of the country of Israel's history from the time of Joshua to the present day. Use a long sheet of paper and perhaps add pictures.

- Create a colorful, trifold travel brochure for the Holy Land, inviting people to visit it. Highlight a few sites that are linked to our Blessed Mother.

- Draw a blueprint of the Temple of Jerusalem, which was the heart of the Jewish faith. Label its courts and important features.

• Write a report on the history of the second Temple of Jerusalem, which replaced Solomon's Temple. Mary spent much time there:

> According to tradition, she lived the early years of her life in the Temple.
> She went there for her purification after the birth of Jesus and to present him to God.
> Her family went to the Temple each year for Passover.
> She found her missing Son there.

• Find out why there is strife in Israel today between the Israelites and Palestinians.

• Write a report on the conflict among religious traditions in the Basilica of the Holy Sepulcher.

Mary's Words and Thoughts

Because our Blessed Mother is an ideal Christian and a model for us, her words and thoughts contain lessons for our spiritual lives.

• Read what Mary said during the Annunciation as recorded in Luke 1:26–38. What do her words reveal about her? What do they teach us?

• Read Mary's prayer, the Magnificat in Luke 1:46–55. Write your own Magnificat.

• Read Mary's words to her Son after discovering him in the Temple. How do they show she is like most mothers?

• Read what Mary said to Jesus and to the servants at the wedding at Cana. What message do they hold for us?

• Consider how Mary meditates in Luke 12:19 and Luke 2:51. Choose an experience you had recently and ponder it. What might God be telling you through it?

Chapter 2

What Scripture Reveals about the Virgin Mary

Saint Jerome famously said, "Ignorance of Scripture is ignorance of Christ." That can be paraphrased to "Ignorance of Scripture is ignorance of Christ's mother." In the Bible God revealed what he wanted us to know about Mary. We may wish that God chose to reveal more about her. Still, the passages in Scripture referring to Mary are significant. They tell us that she is the virgin Mother of God through the power of the Holy Spirit. Moreover, they convey that she is a strong, courageous, holy woman filled with a great love for God and other people.

Interestingly, the Quran, the Muslim holy book, contains forty-two verses about Mary, which is more than the Bible has. In fact, its surah (chapter) nineteen is titled Mary.

Mary in the New Testament

Most of our knowledge about Mary comes from Luke's Gospel, predominantly in the Infancy Narratives of chapters 1 and 2. Perhaps Luke was privileged to hear the details of the birth and childhood of Jesus directly from her. The Gospel of Matthew adds Joseph's side of the story, the visit of the Magi, and the flight into Egypt. In John's Gospel we learn about the wedding at Cana and Mary's presence at the crucifixion. Acts shows us Mary at Pentecost, gathered with the disciples in the upper room. Then nothing more about her life on earth is recounted in Scripture.

Activities

• Choose one Scripture passage about Mary from the list on the next page and read it slowly. As you read, try to visualize the event. Then reflect on what it meant for Mary and what it means for you. Respond with a prayer to our Blessed Mother based on what you read.

Events in Mary's Life

Luke 1:26-38	The Annunciation
Luke 1:39–45	The Visitation
Luke 1:46–55	Mary's Magnificat
Luke 2:1–20	The Nativity
Matthew 2:1–12	Visit of the Magi
Matthew 2:13–23	Flight into Egypt
Luke 2:22–38	The Presentation of Jesus and Purification of Mary
Luke 2:41–51	Finding Jesus in the Temple
John 2:1–10	The Wedding at Cana
John 19:25–27	The Crucifixion
Acts 1:12-14; 2:1–4	Pentecost

• Experience a guided meditation on one of the events above. See the one on the wedding at Cana in **Appendix A** on page 75.

• Illustrate an event in Mary's life by one of these means:

 – Drawing it with pencil, crayons, colored pencils, pastels, black ink, or chalk
 – Painting it with watercolors, oil paint, or acrylic paint
 – Creating a mosaic
 – Making a clay sculpture

• Create a mural of happenings in Mary's life on a long sheet of paper.

• Write a paragraph on what a certain event reveals about Mary's character.

• Tell the story of an event in Mary's life to a younger child or class. Use expression and gestures. Practice before you present the story.

• Explain what you think Mary's life was like after the Church's birth at Pentecost. Remember that Jesus entrusted her to Saint John the apostle as his mother.

• Give a reason why our Blessed Mother might not have died and a reason why she probably did. The Church has not declared her death.

• Prepare an interview with Mary. Plan questions on topics related to Mary and imagine her responses. Write the interview or stage it with another person acting as Mary or the interviewer. Possible topics:

Mary's Son Jesus	The wedding at Cana
The visitation	The neighbors' attempt to kill Jesus
The birth of Jesus	The death of Joseph
The flight into Egypt	The death of Jesus
The visit of the Magi	The resurrection
The prophecy of Simeon	Pentecost
Finding Jesus in the Temple	

• Prepare an interview of someone associated with Mary, such as the Angel Gabriel, Jesus, Joseph, Joachim, Anne, Elizabeth, Simeon, Anna, and Saint John. Write the interview or present it with one of two other persons. See **Appendix B** on page 76 for an example.

• Pretend to be Mary or someone associated with her and deliver a monologue that includes an event the person experienced, how they felt about it, and their hopes for the future.

• Dramatize one or more scenes from Mary's life incorporating words taken from Scripture. You might create a setting and use costumes.

• Make a timeline of Mary's life, perhaps one with pictures.

• Compose a journal entry Mary might have written either on an ordinary day or on a special day.

• Write a piece for the *Nazareth Gazette* about Mary or an event in her life, such as her neighbors' attempt to kill her son or her assistance at the wedding in Cana. You might write a news article, a main feature, or an editorial.

 • Present an event in Mary's life in any of these ways:

Mime	Bulletin board
Shadow play	Tableau
Puppet show	Chalk (or felt-tipped pen) talk
Reader's theater	Dance
Flannel board	

• Purchase or make a Christmas card or a set of cards that picture Mary, the Mother of God, with her Son Jesus.

• Write a story about Mary in the form of a choral reading composed of lines spoken by a narrator, characters, and groups or a chorus. Choose an occurrence in her life as told in Scripture or one of her apparitions. See **Appendix C** on page 77 for an example.

• Create a documentary on Mary as a PowerPoint presentation, radio program, video, or podcast.

• Read Revelation 12:1–6. The woman described is said to symbolize Israel, the Church, or Mary. Explain why the passage can be interpreted as referring to Mary.

• Find or draw a picture of Mary as the woman described in Revelation 12:1–6. She is clothed with the sun, the moon is under her feet, and on her head is a crown of twelve stars.

Mary in the Old Testament

Saint Augustine said that the New Testament is concealed in the Old Testament and the Old is revealed by the New. Certain people, events, and things in the Old Testament prefigure, or foreshadow, people, events, and things in the New Testament and are called types. For example, God giving the Commandments on Mount Sinai prefigures Jesus giving the Beatitudes during his sermon on the mount. The Church sees several places in the Old Testament where Mary is referred to or prefigured.

Activities

• Read Genesis 3:15, the protoevangelium, which means the first Gospel or first good news. Traditionally this verse is believed to refer to Mary, the "new Eve." That is why some images depict her with a serpent (Satan) underfoot. Saint Irenaeus observed, "The knot of Eve's disobedience was untied by Mary's obedience."

• Read one or more of the following passages about people and objects and be ready to tell how these types prefigure the Blessed Virgin.

Sarah	Genesis 17:16; 21:1–2
Jacob's ladder	Genesis 28:12
The burning bush	Exodus 3:1–3
Ark of the Covenant	Exodus 25:21–22
Manna	Exodus 16:13–15
Gideon's fleece	Judges 6:39–40
Eve	Genesis 2:21–23
Sarah	Genesis 1:9–14
Hannah	1 Samuel 1–2:21
Bathsheba	1 Kings 2:13–20
Esther	Book of Esther
Judith	Book of Judith

• Write a poem about one or more Old Testament types of Mary. Choose a form of poetry from the list on pages 53–55.

• Compile a booklet that comprises pages about types of Mary. Include pictures.

• Look up and read Isaiah 7:14, Micah 5:2–3, and Jeremiah 31:22. These passages are interpreted as referring to our Blessed Mother.

Chapter 3

What We Believe about Mary

Information about Mary's life is sparse. No one wrote her biography or took her picture. Plus, the Gospels do not mention her between Jesus' infancy and his finding in the Temple at age twelve, during the twenty or so years before he left for his public ministry, and after Pentecost. Several people, like the mystics Saint Bridget of Sweden, Venerable Mary of Agreda, and Blessed Anne Catherine Emmerich, supply details about Mary that allegedly were revealed to them in visions. Some of these details contradict, for example, how long after Jesus' death Mary was assumed into heaven. The writings of visionaries are deemed private revelations, which means they need not be believed.

We do not know how tall Mary was or whether her eyes were brown or blue. Fortunately, the Holy Spirit—working through Scripture, Tradition, and the Church—has informed us of the essential truths about the mother of the Savior. That knowledge is far more important than knowing her physical characteristics.

Church Teachings

The Church, including the Saints, loved and venerated Mary from early on. Saint Paul referred to her before the Gospels writers did. In a letter he stated, "God sent his Son, born of a woman ... so that we might receive adoption as children" (Galatians 4:4). In 431 at the Council of Ephesus held in the Church of Mary, Mary was officially declared the Theotokos, which is Greek for Mother of God or God Bearer. This is a dogma of the Catholic faith, which means it is infallibly true and must be believed.

Activities

• Read all or some of the paragraphs about Mary in the *Catholic Catechism of the Church,* #484–511 and #963–975.

• Prepare a PowerPoint presentation based on the paragraphs about Mary in the *Catholic Catechism of the Church,* #484–511 and #963–975.

• Draw up eight questions that can be answered in the paragraphs about Mary in the *Catholic Catechism of the Church,* #484–511 and #963–975.

• Read the last chapter of the Second Vatican Council's document on the Church, *Lumen Gentium* (A Light to the Nations), chapter eight, which is about our Blessed Mother. Use the study guide in **Appendix D** on page 76; the answers are on page 83.

• Explain why you think that the council fathers chose to include Mary in the document on the Church. By the way, while Christ is the head of the Church, she has been called its neck!

• Read all or sections of these Church documents on Mary and make a written or oral report on what you read:

  – The United States bishops' pastoral letter "Behold Your Mother" (1973)
  – Pope Saint John Paul II's encyclical *Redemptoris Mater* (Mother of the Redeemer) (1987)
  – Pope Saint Paul VI's encyclical *Marialis Cultis* (Marian Devotion) (1974)

• Find out what the present pope has said about the Virgin Mary in a homily or statement. Write three ideas that impressed you.

• Discover the meaning of the Latin terms *latria, dulia,* and *hyperdulia* as they refer to adoration and veneration.

Mary's Privileges

Because Mary has the exceptional role of Mother of God in salvation history (her greatest privilege), God bestowed on her three special privileges. Through the guidance of the Holy Spirit, the Church proclaimed them dogmas of the Catholic faith. These are the three privileges:

Immaculate conception. Mary was free from all sin from the first moment of her existence by God's special grace. The purging of sin that Jesus won for all of us on the cross was retroactive in her case. Poet William Wordsworth called Mary "our tainted nature's solitary boast."

Perpetual virginity. Jesus was conceived solely by the power of the Holy Spirit. No man was involved. Catholics believe that Jesus was Mary's only child. Where the Gospels refer to his brothers and sisters, those terms might mean "cousins." Or else they could refer to Joseph's children from a previous marriage.

Assumption. When Mary's life on earth came to a close, she was taken to heaven body and soul, as we hope to be someday. The mother of God was not obliged to wait until the end of the world for her body and soul to be reunited.

Activities

• Find out the year that the Church declared each of Mary's three privileges.

• Write a prayer to Mary that is focused on one of her privileges.

• Locate art that depicts Mary's privileges. Here are examples:

Immaculate conception	"The Immaculate Conception" by Diego Velázquez
Perpetual virginity	"The Annunciation" by Henry Ossawa Tanner
Assumption	"The Assumption" by Titian

Mary as Intercessor

Every time we pray the Hail Mary we ask our Blessed Mother to pray for us. As queen mother in heaven, she is a strong ally, a powerful mediator for us with the King. Besides, she loves us and knows our needs. Just as her heart was moved at the Cana wedding to prompt her Son to supply more wine, she is willing and eager to come to our aid.

Numerous stories are told of miracles that resulted from Mary's intercession. According to one legend, during the Middle Ages Europe's crops were plagued by pests. After farmers prayed to Mary, beetles appeared that preserved the crops. These beetles were dubbed ladybugs in honor of Our Lady! Their red color was said to resemble her cloak, and their seven black dots were thought to represent her seven sorrows.

Activities

• Write a report on the miracle attributed to Our Lady of Prompt Succor that occurred during the Battle of New Orleans.

• Learn about the healing miracle that Saint Therese of Lisieux experienced when she was ten years old.

• Find out the meaning and origin of the football expression "Hail Mary pass."

• List your needs and the needs of your loved ones, your country, and the world. Pray a litany in which you state each need and after each one ask, "Mary, pray for me (or us or them)."

• Ask a few people if they have ever prayed to Our Lady for a special intention and if so, was their request answered.

Chapter 4

Mary's Many Titles

Referring to Saint Mary, a Flemish hymn begins "Love gave her a thousand names." Titles bestowed on Mary reflect what we believe about her. From antiquity she has been called Theotokos (bearer of God). We know her as Our Lady, Blessed Virgin Mary, and Blessed Mother. Myriad titles of Mary are based on her qualities and roles or are derived from places where she appeared, for instance, Our Lady of Fatima. A recent new title is Our Lady of Evangelization.

In the Litany of Loreto we address Mary by some lovely titles. In 2020, Pope Francis added three more: Mother of Mercy, Mother of Hope, and Solace of Migrants.

Activities

• Compile a list of Mary's titles. Decide which are your three favorite ones and explain why you like them.

• Discover the story connected with a Marian title. Our Lady Untier (or Undoer) of Knots, a favorite title of Pope Francis, is an interesting one to investigate.

• Come up with your own title for our Blessed Mother, perhaps one that pertains to your life or something in the world today.

• Search for paintings that have given Mary a new title like Our Lady of the Sparrow. These names are derived from the things or people that the artist included in her picture.

• Look for titles that Muslims give Our Lady.

• Choose a title for Mary and compose a prayer based on it.

• Find Latin American countries that honor Mary as their patroness under a particular title. Learn the story behind some of their choices.

• Research why Jesus addressed Mary as woman instead of mother twice: at the wedding in Cana (John 2:4) and from the cross (John 19:26).

• Create an acrostic for a name or title of Mary. List the letters vertically. Then for each one write a phrase or part of a complete sentence that refers to our Blessed Mother and begins with that letter. Here is an example:

Quick to say yes to God
Untouched by sin
Eager to hear the prayers of her children
Everyone's heavenly mother
Now in heaven body and soul with her Son Jesus

An alternate: Set the word or words vertically and place other letters around them to form Marian words or phrases like this acrostic:

coMpassion
fAith
couRage
loyaltY

Chapter 5

Praying to Our Blessed Mother

Every day one-year-old Anna Maria would stand in front of the statue of Mary in the front yard and carry on a conversation in babble language. Her parents had already instilled in her the value of talking to her heavenly mother, in other words, praying to Mary.

We glorify God whenever we honor Mary, his most sublime creation. Just as children like to hear their mother praised, Jesus is pleased whenever we praise his mother. We do not worship Mary; rather we acknowledge the beautiful qualities with which God graced her.

On Calvary when Jesus bequeathed his mother to the apostle John, he was also giving her to us as our loving mother who is concerned for us. So we turn to Mary for support when we are in need. You might wonder, Why not take our petitions directly to God? Asking our heavenly mother to plead on our behalf is comparable to asking our earthly mother, a friend, or another person to pray for us. God will certainly respond positively to his mother's prayers if they are ultimately for the good of all.

Prayers to Mary

Christians have prayed to our Blessed Mother ever since the early days of the Church. After the Our Father, the most well-known prayer is the Hail Mary (Ave Maria in Latin). The first part of this beloved Marian prayer is taken from Scripture. It begins with the Angel Gabriel's words to the teenage Mary at the annunciation: "Hail Mary, full of grace, the Lord is with you" (Luke 1:28). This is followed by Elizabeth's greeting to her at the visitation: "Blessed are you among women and blessed is the fruit of your womb" (Luke 1:41–42). The Church added the word *Jesus* and the rest of the prayer.

Activities

• Adopt the tradition of praying three Hail Marys every morning or evening or both. This practice is said to be in honor of the Trinity: the power of the Father, the wisdom of the Holy Spirit, and the mercy of the Son. Others hold that it honors Mary's power, wisdom, and mercy.

• Think of gestures to add to the words of the Hail Mary as you pray it. Or learn to pray this prayer in American Sign Language by finding an example on youTube.

• Learn how to pray the Hail Mary in another language like Spanish, French, or Latin.

• Compile a booklet of Marian prayers like those listed here. Add pictures if you wish.

Memorare – Remember, O Most gracious Virgin . . .

We Fly to Thy Patronage (*Sub Tuum Praesidium*) – The oldest Marian prayer

Angelus – Formerly prayed morning, noon, and evening when church bells rang

Regina Caeli – Queen of Heaven

Salve Regina – Hail, Queen

Ave Maris Stella – Hail, Star of the Sea

Magnificat – Mary's prayer when she visited Elizabeth

Consecration to Mary – My Queen and my Mother, . . .

Alma Redemptoris Mater – Loving Mother of the Redeemer

• Memorize a Marian prayer. Here are three methods:

 – Write phrases of the prayer on flashcards or strips of paper. Scramble them and then arrange them in order.
 – Draw jigsaw puzzle pieces on heavy paper, making as many pieces as there are phrases. Write a phrase on each piece in order. Cut out the pieces and mix them up. Put the puzzle together.
 – Write the words of the prayer on the links of a paper chain and hang it where you will see it.

• Write an original prayer to Mary.

• Look up the Common of the Blessed Virgin in a Divine Office prayer book (also called Liturgy of the Hours and Prayer of Christians) and pray its intercessions and concluding prayer.

• Learn about the Little Office of the Blessed Virgin Mary and write a report on it. You might also pray it.

• Find a version of Mary's Stations of the Cross and pray it, especially during Lent.

• Locate the prayer the Divine Praises and pray aloud the lines that refer to Mary.

• Choose one of the beautiful titles of Mary from the Litany of Loreto title and write a reflection based on it.

• Find a litany to the Blessed Virgin Mary other than the Litany of Loreto and pray it. Here are a few possibilities:

   Litany of the Holy Name of Mary
   Litany of the Immaculate Heart of Mary
   Litany of the Immaculate Conception
   Litany of Our Lady of Seven Sorrows
   Litany of Mary of Nazareth

• Under a variety of titles Mary is the patroness of all fifty states in the United States. See Elizabeth Scalia's Litany to the Immaculate Conception, Patroness of the United States of America at https://bit.ly/3irBZAY.

• Compose your own litany of Our Lady. You might make up original titles for her such as those found in the Litany of Mary of Nazareth.

• Find out how many Masses in honor of the Blessed Virgin Mary the Congregation of Divine Worship published.

• Find a prayer to Mary composed by one of the saints and pray it. An example would be Saint Francis of Assisi's Salutation of the Blessed Virgin Mary.

• Locate and pray one of the novenas to Our Lady. A novena is praying a certain prayer for nine consecutive days. This practice recalls the nine days Mary and the apostles spent praying in the upper room before Pentecost.

• Explore Marian chaplets other than the Rosary. A chaplet is a prayer prayed on beads. The number of beads and the prayers prayed on chaplets vary. One example is the Chaplet of the Immaculate Conception created by Saint John Berchmans, S.J., to preserve purity. It has three sets of four beads separated by three Our Father beads. A Miraculous Medal of the Immaculate Conception is attached to it.

• Prepare a prayer service to celebrate our Blessed Mother. Include Marian prayers and hymns, Scripture passages and other readings about her, a brief talk, and time for private reflection.

• Organize and carry out the prayer service on Mary's "garden of virtues" found in **Appendix H** on page 83.

• Read this selection from a homily of Saint Bernard of Clairvaux:

> In danger, in anguish, in uncertainty, think of Mary, call on Mary. May she never be far from your lips, from your heart; and thus you will be able to obtain the help of her prayers, never forget the example of her life. If you follow her, you cannot go astray; if you pray to her, you cannot despair; if you think of her, you cannot be mistaken. If she sustains you, you cannot fall; if she protects you, you have nothing to fear; if she guides you, you do not tire; if she shows you favor, you will reach the goal.

• Use the devotional *Heart to Heart with Mary* by Mary Kathleen Glavich, SND. In it our Blessed Mother speaks lovingly to you personally as her child each day of the year.

• Collect Marian aspirations, one-line prayers like "My mother, my hope," listing them in your homemade prayer book or on a computer document. Pray at least one of them frequently.

Consecration to Mary

Consecration, or entrustment to Mary, not only expresses love for her but is a way of going to Jesus through her. It entrusts a person or country to Our Lady for guidance and protection. The notion of belonging to Mary first appeared in the fourth century. Saint Pope John Paul II, who had a great love for Mother Mary, expressed his consecration to her in his papal motto: *Totus Tuus* (Totally Yours).

Activities

• Pray a version of a prayer of consecration to Mary.

• Research the history of consecration to Mary.

• Find out about a longer process of consecration to Mary such as Saint Louis de Montfort and Saint Maximilian Kolbe taught.

Hymns about or to Mary

Saint Augustine claimed, "Singing well is praying twice." Lovers of Mary have composed chants, antiphons, ballads, carols, and other songs about her. Numerous composers have created musical settings for the Ave Maria, Magnificat, and Stabat Mater. Arguably the most well-known Marian hymn is "O Sanctissima," which was first published in 1792 and thought to have originated with Sicilian seamen invoking Mary's protection each evening. A traditional favorite is "On This Day, O Beautiful Mother" composed by Louis Lambillotte (1796-1855).

Activities

- Choose a Marian hymn from a hymnal or youTube and write an explanation of its words. What truths does it convey and celebrate?

- Listen to a recording of a Marian hymn and make it your prayer. You might select "O Sanctissima," "Hail Mary, Gentle Woman," or one of the many arrangements of the Magnificat.

- Compose a hymn in honor of Mary. Write original music or set words to another song's melody.

- Play a musical arrangement of a prayer to Mary on a musical instrument. Possibilities are Schubert's "Ave Maria" or Carey Landry's "Hail Mary: Gentle Woman."

- Listen to a contemporary Christian song about Mary on youTube, for example, Amy Grant's "Breath of Heaven."

- List Christmas carols that focus on Mary or mention her. Listen to or sing at least one of them.

- Find and read all the verses of the thirteenth-century hymn "Stabat Mater Dolorosa" (The Sorrowful Mother Stood). This hymn is the optional sequence for the feast of Our Lady of Sorrows and is sometimes sung during the Stations of the Cross.

- Create gestures or a dance to accompany and interpret a Marian hymn.

- Prepare a program that tells the story of Mary's life and incorporates Marian hymns. Present the program to another family, class, or parish group.

- Locate and read the Eastern Christian Church's "Akathist Hymn: Salutations to the Mother of God" composed in the seventh century. It addresses Our Lady by dozens of titles. People customarily stand during this lengthy hymn.

Chapter 6

The Rosary, a Special Prayer

John Smillie drew a cartoon titled "The First Rosary." It shows the child Jesus tugging on Mary's robe and saying, "Mama, mama, mama." The cartoon captures in a playful way the essence of the Rosary. In this prayer we call on our Blessed Mother no less than fifty-three times as we pray the Hail Marys.

Although the Rosary really didn't originate with Jesus, it has a long history. The word *bead* is from the old English word *bede,* which means "prayer." For hundreds of years people of different faiths have prayed on strings of beads. The Catholic rosary is the most well-known. As the name rosary implies, praying it is like presenting a garland of roses to Our Lady. Saint Padre Pio observed, "In times of darkness, holding the rosary beads is like holding your Blessed Mother's hand."

Facts about the Rosary

A tradition exists that the Rosary began when Mary personally gave it to Saint Dominic (1170–1221). If she did, it was not in the form we know it today. Even the Hail Mary prayer had not yet been fully composed. Whether or not the commonly accepted tradition is true, under Saint Dominic's leadership, the Dominicans zealously promoted the Rosary.

The rosary is a beloved prayer. Rosaries are seen hanging from rearview mirrors, worn around the neck, and in the hands of the deceased. Children may receive a rosary as a First Communion gift. Rosaries that are blessed by a priest or deacon become sacramentals.

NOTE: Rosary is capitalized when it refers to the prayer and lowercase when it stands for the beads.

Activities

• Research the history of the Rosary. Discover its origin, how it evolved, and times Our Lady appeared and urged us to pray it. Find out why the Rosary is called Mary's Psalter.

• Learn how the Battle of Lepanto in 1571 is connected to the Rosary.

• Design a poster that illustrates how to pray the Rosary. Draw a rosary and label the prayers prayed on the beads.

• Memorize the Joyful, Luminous, Sorrowful, and Glorious Mysteries of the Rosary found in **Appendix E** on page 79 with their Scripture references. Pray them on their traditional days:

Joyful Mysteries: Monday, Saturday, and Sundays during Advent
Luminous Mysteries: Thursday
Sorrowful Mysteries: Tuesday, Friday, and Sundays during Lent
Glorious Mysteries: Sunday and Wednesday

• Make a booklet about the mysteries of the Rosary: Joyful, Luminous, Sorrowful, and Glorious. Or make four booklets, one for each set of mysteries. See why the Rosary is the Gospel on beads.

• Create your own mysteries such as five parables of Jesus, five miracles of Jesus, or five events in your life. Pray a Rosary using your original mysteries.

• Find out how the assassination attempt on Pope Saint John Paul II in 1981 is associated with Our Lady of Fatima and what he did with one of the bullets. Tell someone the story.

• Investigate how important the Rosary was to famous people like Louis Pasteur, Martin Luther, and Joseph Haydn.

• Read Pope Saint John Paul II's apostolic letter on the Rosary, "*Rosarium Virginis Mariae*" (The Rosary of the Virgin Mary). Write a summary of it.

• Ask people you know if they pray the Rosary and if so, why, when, and how they pray it. Report your findings.

• Write a short biography of Father Patrick Peyton, C.S.C., who is known as "The Rosary Priest" because he zealously promoted praying the Rosary.

• Look up paintings of "Our Lady of the Rosary," in particular, Bartolomé Esteban Murillo's, which was painted around 1640. Which one do you like best?

Making a Rosary

Prayer beads originally were pebbles, bits of bone, or berries on a string. Today's rosaries range from knots on a cord to a circlet of gems. The beads may be plastic, wood, glass, or crystal. Some rosaries are made of pressed rose petals and give off a lovely scent.

Activities

• Produce a rosary in a creative way, for example, by using bread dough, noodles, or crushed rose petals for beads. One school held a contest asking families to make a unique rosary. The winning rosary was made of washers and corks.

• Make a rosary with children by placing items of food like cheerios, raisins, grapes, miniature marshmallows, or candy pieces on a flat surface to represent the beads. Add a crucifix or a cookie shaped like a cross.

• Make a rosary by stringing beads or knotting a cord. Directions for making a knotted rosary are at https://rosaryarmy.com. For supplies see Our Lady's Rosary Makers at https://www.olrm.org and other sites on the Internet.

• Begin a rosary-making group in your home or parish. Rosaries can be donated to missions.

• Fashion a rosary case out of a rectangle of heavy fabric about four inches wide. Close it with a short zipper or Velcro.

Praying the Rosary

Notable people, including countless saints, prayed the Rosary. It was Pope Saint John Paul II's favorite prayer. In the eleventh century Lady Godiva bequeathed her paternoster of precious gems to a monastery. This paternoster, a forerunner of the rosary, was a circle of beads on which Our Fathers were prayed. *Pater noster* is Latin for "our father."

Activities

• Ask a priest or deacon to bless a new rosary.

• Teach a child how to pray the Rosary.

• Pray the Rosary at various times:

– While walking, running, exercising, swimming, waiting in a doctor's office
– While traveling by car, bus, train, or plane
– As you carry out a monotonous chore like folding laundry or cutting the lawn
– When you have a hard time falling asleep, the Rosary's rhythm may lull you to sleep.
– While waiting for something to download or when put on hold on the phone

• Make the outline of a rosary in yarn on a bulletin board or draw it with felt-tipped pen on a poster board or large sheet of paper. Indicate the beads by small dots. Cut circles from colored paper to represent the beads and distribute them to the participants. Take turns praying the Rosary prayers and affixing the beads in place with pins or glue.

• Pray the Rosary as a family. Father Patrick Peyton, C.S.C., coined the expression "The family that prays together stays together." He began the Family Rosary Crusade movement.

• Think of five original mysteries of the Rosary that are related to Mary. These may be her titles or roles she has. Then pray a Rosary using your new mysteries.

• Pray a scriptural Rosary that includes Bible passages related to each mystery. These can be found on the Internet and in book such as *Scriptural Rosaries in Verse* by Mary Doreen Strahler, SND.

• View art depicting the mysteries as you pray the Rosary. See the book *Mysteries Made Visible: Praying the Rosary with Sacred Art* by Fr. Lawrence Lew, O.P.

• Pray along with a Rosary as it is prayed on a CD, an app, or a video on youTube. One site is www.comepraytherosary.org.

• Vary ways of praying the decades. Here are a few ideas:

  – Offer each decade for an intention or a person.
  – Stay mindful of the mystery by inserting words that refer to it into the Hail Marys. For example, for the first joyful mystery, the Annunciation, you might pray, "Hail Mary, full of grace, to whom the Angel Gabriel came, the Lord . . ."
  – Visualize each mystery before praying its decade or use a booklet that pictures the mysteries.
  – Pause a bit after you name each mystery.
  – Sing some of the prayers in the Rosary.
  – Keep focused on the prayers, by praying them aloud or in a whisper.

– After each decade pray the prayer that Mary gave the three children who saw her in Fatima:

O my Jesus,
forgive us our sins,
save us from the fires of hell,
and lead all souls to heaven,
especially those in most need of thy mercy.

• Carry out a living Rosary:

– Children (and perhaps adults) representing Hail Mary and Our Father beads stand in a circle outside or in a church, forming five decades. Five children who lead the Apostles' Creed and other introductory prayers stand in a line perpendicular to the first "decade." One child may stand at the head and carry a large crucifix.

– Before each decade, its mystery is announced, followed by a reflection, skit, tableau, poem, cheer, or hymn.

– Using a microphone, the participants take turns praying the first part of their prayer. They might carry flowers and at the conclusion of their prayer place them in a vase before an image of Mary. Those who pray the Our Father might carry a vigil light or candle to be lit there.

• Pray the Rosary using a one-decade strand, bracelet, finger ring with ten knobs, or keychain.

• When no rosary is available, pray on your ten fingers.

• Read a book about the Rosary.

Chapter 7

Other Marian Devotions

We love Mary because her yes to God led to our salvation. We also love her because she is our heavenly mother who loves us and prays for us. A fanciful story tells of Jesus chiding Peter, the keeper of heaven's gates, "Why are there so many sinners in heaven? You were supposed to close the gates on them." Peter replied, "I did close the gates, but your mother opened the window."

Love for Mary has given birth to a variety of devotions. Through them we honor her because she had the unique and astounding privilege of being the Mother of God. Devotions may be prayers or actions. Some are worldwide, like the Rosary. Others are local, like the celebration of the feast of Saint Mary the Crowned of Carmel (otherwise known as Our Lady of the Hens) in the Italian town of Pagani. The Church has pointed out that devotions should be tied to the liturgy, which is far more important.

Times for Honoring Mary

The Church has dedicated the months of the year and the days of the week to certain religious mysteries and persons. It's no surprise that some of these times center on our Blessed Mother.

Activities

• Do something special to honor Mary during May, her month, and on Saturdays, her day, and on one or more of her feast days, which are listed on pages 43–44. For example, you might place freshly cut flowers before her statue in your church or home.

• Take up or renew the practice of praying the Rosary in October, the month of the Rosary.

• Learn about the First Saturday devotion and consider practicing it.

• Find out what is meant by a Marian year and when the last two international ones occurred.

• Carry out a "Mary Day." You might include a multimedia presentation, Scripture, prayers, readings about Mary, and hymns. Participants could wear something blue, which traditionally is Mary's color.

May Devotions

In the northern hemisphere, May is the lovely spring month when earth comes to life again after a cold, barren winter when many trees and flowers appear to be dead and animals hibernate. Spring is a fitting time to celebrate the beautiful mother whose Son offers us eternal life. Mary is fittingly called Queen of May.

Activities

• Set up a "Mary altar" during the month of May in your classroom or home. On it place a lovely cloth or doily, an image of Mary, a rosary, a candle, and flowers. Pray before it each day in May. You might keep this shrine up all year.

• Hold a May Crowning that includes readings from Scripture, Marian hymns, and prayers. Find or make a crown, perhaps out of flowers. Make sure that it fits the statue of Mary that will be crowned. Choose someone to carry the crown on a cushion and place it on the statue. A step ladder might be needed. First Communicants could wear their First Communion dresses or suits.

• Participate in a procession to a statue or shrine of Mary. On the way and at the shrine sing Marian hymns and pray Marian prayers like the Rosary.

Advent Devotions

The three main figures of Advent are Isaiah the prophet, John the Baptist, and the Blessed Virgin. Of these people, Mary, who carried Jesus for nine months before his birth, is the dominant one. During Advent we try to imitate Mary's joyful, prayerful preparation and expectant longing for the Savior to come into the world. We long for his second coming.

Activities

• Celebrate these three Marian feasts that occur during Advent: Immaculate Conception, December 8; Our Lady of Loreto, December 10; and Our Lady of Guadalupe, December 12.

• Spend Advent conscious of Mary awaiting the birth of her Son. Mark a white pillar candle with a symbol for Jesus such as a chi-rho. Represent Mary by wrapping a blue or white cloth like a mantle around the candle. On Christmas remove the cloth and light the candle.

• Carry out the traditional practice of "harboring Mary" throughout Advent. Pin a Marian medal under your clothes or wear one around your neck.

• Participate in a posada. People process to a different house each night in remembrance of Mary and Joseph's search for an inn. The visits occur over the nine days before Christmas to represent the nine months Mary was pregnant. They can include a prayer service and a celebration in each house. People may enact the roles of Mary, Joseph, and the innkeeper.

Sacramentals

Sacramentals are blessings or objects through which grace is bestowed by the prayers and merits of the Church. Sacramentals are related to the sacraments, but unlike sacraments their effects depend on the attitude of the person using them. The rosary is a sacramental related to Mary. Certain scapulars and the Miraculous Medal are two others.

Activities

• Research the origin and meaning of the Brown Scapular of Our Lady of Mount Carmel. Obtain this scapular, in either its cloth or metal form, and ask a priest to bless it. Then be invested in the scapular and enrolled in the Confraternity of the Brown Scapular.

• Among the seventeen scapulars approved by the Church are a few others in honor of Mary besides the brown Scapular of Mount Carmel. Find out what these are.

• Learn about the history, design, and purpose of the Miraculous Medal. Begin wearing one.

• Find images of medals in honor of Mary other than the Miraculous Medal. Purchase one for yourself and wear it, especially on her feast days.

Seven Sorrows and Seven Joys

At the presentation of Jesus in the Temple, Simeon said to Mary, "A sword will pierce your own soul too" (Luke 2:35). Tradition honors seven sorrowful events in Mary's life. In some art seven swords pierce her heart. Devotion to the Mary's joys predates devotion to her seven sorrows.

Activities

• List what you think are Mary's traditional seven sorrows and seven joys. Then find out how close you were to being correct.

• Write a reflection on one of Mary's sorrows or joys.

• Find out what the Franciscan Crown Rosary is, then pray it.

• Research the history of devotion to the seven sorrows of Mary.

• Find out how to pray the Seven Sorrows Chaplet and pray it.

• Locate the Litany of the Seven Sorrows and pray it.

• Write a psalm of lament that Mary could have composed after her Son's death.

• Write a psalm of praise and thanks that Mary could have composed after the birth of Jesus or after his resurrection.

• Identify Mary's sorrows and joys other than the traditional ones.

Mary Garden

For centuries people have planted Mary gardens where flowers and herbs related to her grow. Some plants in them symbolize our Blessed Mother, for instance, the rose. Others are compared to her features like the lily-of-the-valley (Mary's tears) or things that belong to her like the cornflower (Mary's crown).

Activities

• Research flowers and herbs that are fitting for a Mary garden and compile a list. Tell how each one is connected to the Blessed Virgin.

• Grow a Mary garden at your home, school, or parish. Set a statue or picture of Mary in it.

• Plant a miniature Mary garden in your house or on your patio or balcony. Grow the flowers and herbs in a planter or terrarium.

• Find out if there is a Mary garden that you can visit and then do so.

• Pray the Garden of Virtues prayer service in **Appendix H** on page 83.

Traveling Mary Statue

The custom of taking turns hosting a statue of Mary originated with the story of Mary and Joseph being turned away from the inns at Bethlehem. This gave rise to the German custom of *Frauentragen* (the carrying of Mary) and later the posada (shelter) of Spanish-speaking countries. (See page 37 for an explanation of the posada tradition.) The most popular traveling statue is Our Lady of Fatima, which has been welcomed in homes since 1947. These are two other examples of traveling Mary statues:

In Italy beginning in 2011, a statue of Mary of the Miraculous Medal went from parish to parish to mark the anniversary of Mary's apparition to Saint Catherine Labouré.

In 2022 the statue Mary, Mother of God began a yearlong pilgrimage to churches, schools, and other institutions in the diocese of Charlotte, North Carolina, to mark the 50th anniversary of the diocese.

Activities

• Participate in a parish or school program that involves keeping a statue or other image of Mary in your home for one or more days. Each day the family gathers at the statue for a brief Marian prayer service.

• Initiate the practice of a traveling Mary statue or image in your parish, school, organization, or among people you know.

• Obtain a pocket statue of Mary. Keep this miniature statue with you to remind you of your Blessed Mother during the day.

• Write a report on the traveling statue of Our Lady of Fatima.

Other Marian Activities

• Make a Mary candle and display it on her feast days and
during May. Wrap a blue ribbon around a white pillar
candle. Decorate the candle with Marian symbols like an *M,*
a lily, or a crown by any of these methods:

   – Etch the symbols using a nail, scissor point, or screwdriver
   dipped in hot water.
   – Press colored pushpins into the candle.
   – Spread Mod Podge on the candle where paper symbols
   will go, apply the symbols, and coat them with another
   layer of glue.

• Read a biography of a saint known for having a great love of Mary. An outstanding one is the
Franciscan Saint Maximilian Kolbe who promoted devotion to the Immaculate Virgin Mary.
These are others:

Saint Alphonsus Liguori	Saint John Vianney
Saint Louis de Montfort	Saint Therese of Lisieux
Saint Alexis Falconieri	Saint Bonaventure
Saint Bernard of Clairvaux	Saint Teresa of Calcutta
Saint Padre Pio	Saint Pope John Paul II

• Read the encyclical *Ad Caeli Reginam* (On Proclaiming the Queen of Heaven), which can be
found at https://www.papalencyclicals.net/pius12/p12caeli.htm. Answer this question: Why can
we call Mary the Queen of Heaven and Earth? Through this encyclical of 1954, Pope Pius XII
officially declared Mary the Queen of Heaven and Earth and established the Feast of the
Queenship of Mary.

• Investigate one of the organizations listed here whose members are devoted to Mary and write a report on it.

Legion of Mary

Blue Army of Our Lady of Fatima (world Apostolate of Fatima

International Consecrated Marian Society

Militia Immaculata

Mariological Society of Mary

Marian Movement of Priests

• Find out people and places for whom Mary is the patron saint. List fifteen of these.

Chapter 8

Feasts of Our Lady

A religious community's director of religious formation was dismayed when a candidate showed up for breakfast with his hair dyed blue. "Oh, no!" the director thought. "He's a character we don't need here." But the young man explained, "I dyed it in honor of Mary's feast day today."

Certain days of the liturgical year are designated to honor Mary. The Church has celebrated Marian feasts from its earliest days. New ones have been established recently. In 2018 Pope Francis added the feast of Mary, Mother of the Church to the liturgical calendar. The following year he instituted the feast of Our Lady of Loreto. On Marian feasts, besides going to Mass, the faithful might process through the streets with a statue of Mary, hold parties, or wear a Marian-themed article of clothing.

Praise given to the Mother of God is known as veneration not worship. Therefore, Catholics are not idolators as some people assume. Honoring Mary pleases her Son.

Solemnities

Solemnity of Mary, Holy Mother of God	January 1
The Annunciation of Our Lord	March 25
Assumption	August 15
Immaculate Conception	December 8

Feasts

Visitation of the Blessed Virgin Mary	July 31
The Nativity of the Blessed Virgin Mary	September 8
Our Lady of Guadalupe	December 12

Obligatory Memorials

Mary, Mother of the Church	Monday after Pentecost
Queenship of Mary	August 22
Our Lady of Sorrows	September 15
Our Lady of the Rosary	October 7
Presentation of Mary	November 21

Optional Memorials

Our Lady of Lourdes	February 11
The Immaculate Heart of Mary	Saturday after the Second Sunday after Pentecost
Our Lady of Fatima	May 13
Our Lady of Mount Carmel	July 16
Dedication of Saint Mary Major	August 5
Most Holy Name of the Blessed Virgin Mary	September 12
Our Lady of Loreto	December 10

Two other major feast days are related to Mary:

The Feast of the Holy Family, the Sunday after Christmas

The Feast of the Epiphany, between January 2 and 8.

Three Marian feasts are holy days of obligation: the Solemnity of Mary, the Assumption of the Blessed Virgin Mary, and the Immaculate Conception of the Blessed Virgin Mary.

The Maronite Church celebrates three unique Marian feasts that link Mary to the Eucharist. The names of these feasts are ingredients for bread and wine.

Our Lady of the Seeds	January 15
Our Lady of the Harvest	May 15
Our Lady of the Grapes	August 15

Activities

- Celebrate Marian days on the Church calendar by going to Mass or praying special prayers to her, for example, a Rosary.

- Write a three-to-five-minute homily on Mary based on one of her feasts. Practice it and then deliver it to your family or class.

- Mark Marian days on your calendar with a capital *M* so you remember to celebrate them.

- In a missal or the Divine Office (Prayer of Christians), look up and read the prayers for one or more of Mary's feasts.

- Join a procession in honor of Mary if a parish near you holds one to celebrate one of her feasts. Or process to a shrine in your yard or school. On the way you might sing a Marian hymn or pray the Rosary. At the shrine pray a prayer to our Blessed Mother.

- For any Marian feast, but especially for her birthday on September 8, bake a cake or cookies and decorate them with something that symbolizes Mary like roses, a lily, a fleur-de-lis, a crown, the letter *M*, blue icing, or blue sugar crystals.

  - To make a cake in the shape of an *M,* cut three strips lengthwise in a rectangular cake, then cut one strip in half, and arrange the four pieces to form the letter.
  - Use a bundt cake pan to make a cake in the shape of a crown in honor of Mary. Decorate it with white icing, blue icing, or blueberries.

- For breakfast on a Marian feast serve blueberry muffins or blueberry pancakes.

- Write a radio or television broadcast about a Marian feast. You might deliver it over the school public address system.

• Do something to show love for your heavenly Mother on Mother's Day, which is celebrated on the second Sunday of May. Say a special prayer to her, display her image in a prominent place, set flowers or a plant by her image, or imitate one of her virtues.

• Search for some of the lesser feasts of Mary, for example, Feast of our Lady of Mercy and Feast of our Lady of the Miraculous Medal.

Chapter 9

Mary Portrayed in Art

For centuries Mary has been a favorite subject of painters and sculptors. Arguably the most famous and beloved piece of Marian art is Michelangelo's "Pietà," created in 1498-1499, when he was only twenty-three years old. Sculpted from a piece of Cararra marble, it is a poignant depiction of the bereaved Mary holding her crucified Son on her lap. The artist explained that Mary appears young in order to reflect her purity. Jesus looks peaceful; no signs of his agony remain. The statue can be seen in St. Peter's Basilica in Rome behind bulletproof glass.

The 90-foot statue of Our Lady of the Rockies is the largest one of her in the United States. A 33-foot-high statue in Windsor, Ohio, is the largest one of Our Lady of Guadalupe. No doubt the 322-foot statue Mother of All Asia Tower of Peace in the Philippines is the tallest one of Mary.

Activities

• Locate early images of Mary, especially the oldest one of her and Jesus, which is in the catacomb of Priscilla, and the icon of her that Saint Luke is said to have painted.

• Investigate why Mary is usually pictured clothed in blue or red and with a halo.

• Survey various paintings and statues of Mary on the Internet or in a book. Choose one and decide what characteristic or role of Mary the artist was highlighting. For example, in some paintings Mary's mantle enfolds a multitude of people to show that she protects us, her children.

• Collect images of Mary and display them in a cabinet or on a table or shelf.

- Assemble a quilt of various images of Mary on a large sheet of paper or fabric.

- Prepare a PowerPoint presentation of Marian art. You might take photos of Marian images yourself and use them for this project.

- Search for pictures of Mary that represent different cultures and races like an Asian Mary, a Black Mary, and a Native American Mary.

- Learn about the statue of Our Lady of the Rockies in Montana and write a report about it. Include the story of how it was constructed.

- Find out how icons, which originated in the Eastern Church, differ from other forms of art. Investigate icons of Mary. Select one and tell what aspects of it symbolize, such as the colors, positions, and objects. You might choose arguably the most well-known icon Our Lady of Perpetual Help.

- Find out why some Marian pictures like the painting of Our Lady of Czestochowa are called Black Madonnas. Look for examples.

- Collect pictures of Mary from holy cards, Christmas cards, and magazines. Arrange them in a photo album or scrapbook.

- Explore postage stamps that picture Mary that are issued in the United States or other countries. Which stamp is your favorite?

Art Projects

• Draw, paint, or use clay to create your own depiction of Mary. Make her as beautiful as you can.

• Portray Mary and events in her life using media such as fingerpaint, crayon on sandpaper, torn paper, yarn and cloth, pen and ink, chalk, pastels, and aluminum foil.

• Design a postage stamp in honor of our Blessed Mother. You might base it on one of her titles, an event in her life, or a Marian feast day.

• Create a Marian jigsaw puzzle. Draw straight-lined or interlocking puzzle pieces on the back of a piece of tagboard. On the front of the tagboard, color or paint a picture of Mary or an event in her life. Cut apart the pieces and store them in a box, plastic bag, or an envelope.

• Make a Marian mosaic on stiff paper. Outline a picture such as a rose for Mary, Mystical Rose. For tiles use small, colored pieces cut from construction paper or magazines, paper punch holes, eggshells, seeds, beans, noodles, or rice. Arrange the pieces to fill the design and glue them.

• Create a coat of arms for Mary in the shape of a shield. On it draw symbols that stand for her. Incorporate her colors. Below the coat of arms add a saying that applies to Our Lady.

• Construct a diorama of a Marian event using a box standing on its side. Paint the inside of the box or line it with paper. Draw or paint a setting on the inside back. Place miniature figures in front of the setting. These may be purchased, made from clay or dough, or drawn on stiff paper, cut out, and glued down. Items can also be suspended with string.

• Make a Marian mobile. A simple one can be made with a coat hanger and yarn. Possible themes:

  – The nativity with pictures of Mary, Joseph, Jesus in manger, stable, shepherds, angel, star, three kings
  – Symbols of Mary: a rose, lily, fleur-de-lis, crown, tower, the dawn, a star, fountain, wheatsheaf, mirror, and the letter M
  – Virtues of Mary

• Design a bulletin board in honor of Mary in your home, classroom, or school hall.

• Build a model of a scene from Mary's life or one of her apparitions. Use the lid of a box or a piece of Styrofoam as the stage. Form figures from paper, cardboard, clay, or dough.

• Create a sculpture of Mary or a Marian event using wire, aluminum foil, clay, dough, or papier-mâché.

• Make a Mary doll. Dress one to resemble her, sew or crochet a doll, or make one from a wooden clothespin. Directions can be found on the Internet.

• Make a rose or a carnation from tissue paper and a lily from regular white paper. See **Appendix F** on page 80 for directions. These three flowers are especially associated with Our Lady:

- A rose, known as the queen of flowers, is a symbol for Mary who is called "mystical rose" in the Litany of Loreto.
- Carnations sprang up where Mary's tears fell during her Son's passion according to legend.
- A white lily stands for Mary's purity and beauty. Its golden anthers represent her royalty and the radiance of her soul.

• Make any of these art projects with a Marian theme:

Banner	Collage	Rock paperweight
Doorknob hanger	Button	Flag
Plaque	Cartoon	Suncatcher
Poster	Placemat	Magnet
Stained-glass window	Holy card	Bookmark
Tryptich (three panels)	Bumper sticker	Postcard

• Make a snow globe of Mary.

- Glue a waterproof statue of Mary onto the inside of a jar's lid with a hot glue gun, or place florist clay or modeling clay onto the lid and insert the statue into it.
- Fill the jar with water to within ½" of the top and add glitter, small pieces of eggshells, or confetti. Adding a little glycerin or baby oil to the water will slow the movement of the glitter.
- Screw the lid on tightly. (You might place glue around the threaded rim of the jar and lid first.) If you wish, glue felt onto the top of the lid and tie a ribbon around the jar.

Chapter 10

Mary's Presence in Literature

Did you know that Mary is a main character in one of the Brothers Grimm fairy tales? The bizarre story is called "Our Lady's Child." Our Blessed Mother has been the subject of much literature other than that fairy tale. She appears in prose and poetry, fiction and nonfiction from all nations. Geoffrey Chaucer's writing alone contains about five hundred lines that are Marian poetry. (See his poem "An ABC" –The Prayer of Our Lady.) Dante's *Divine Comedy* includes a lengthy prayer to her. Saints and theologians throughout the ages have written sermons and essays about our Blessed Mother. Saint Anselm noted, "There is never enough said or written about Mary."

Activities

• Read a book about our Blessed Mother and then tell someone about it or write a book report. Here are a few suggestions:

The World's First Love (Archbishop Fulton J. Sheen)

True Devotion to Mary and *The Secret of Mary* (Saint Louis de Montfort)

The Glories of Mary (Saint Alphonsus Liguori)

Reed of God (Caryll Houselander)

The Catholic Companion to Mary (Mary Kathleen Glavich, SND)

The Healing Touch of Mary: Real Life Stories from Those Touched by Mary (Cheri Lomonte)

Truly Our Sister: A Theology of Mary in the Communion of Saints (Elizabeth A. Johnson)

Hail Holy Queen: The Mother of God in the Word of God (Scott Hahn)

Our Lady of the Lost and Found: A Novel of Mary, Faith, and Friendship (Diane Schoemperlen)

Activity books for children:

> *Mother Mary* (Deborah C. Johnson)
>
> *The Story of Mary, Mother of Jesus* (Brother Francis team members)
>
> *Enriching Faith: Lessons, Prayers, and Activities on Mary* (Mary Kathleen Glavich, SND)

• Locate and read a poem about Mary such as these:

"The Virgin" by William Wordsworth

"Lovely Lady Dressed in Blue" by Mary Dixon Thayer, a favorite poem for years

"The Blessed Virgin Compared to the Air We Breathe" and "The May Magnificat" by Gerard Manley Hopkins, S.J.

"The Mother of God" by William Butler Yeats

One of the fourth-century Marian poems by Saint Ephrem the Syrian, who was known as "Mary's Own Singer"

One of the many Marian poems that the Trappist Thomas Merton wrote

• Find and read the poem or hymn "Mary the Dawn." Through beautiful imagery it illustrates Mary's role of presenting Christ to the world. The poem is probably from the Middle Ages, and in the twentieth century Justin Mulcahy, C.P., set the text to music.

Writing Projects

• Compose a poem to or about Our Lady using one of the following forms.

Free verse

A poem that has no set rhyme or rhythm

Ballad

A poem that tells a story, usually in rhymed quatrains (four lines each)

Ode

A poem addressing and praising an object, event, or a person and reflects the writer's feelings toward the subject

Haiku

A three-line poem usually of seventeen syllables:

The first line has 5 syllables; the second line, 7; and the third line, 5.

Sonnet

A fourteen-line poem usually in iambic pentameter.

(This means that each line has five feet that contain one unstressed syllable and one stressed syllable: ta-DUM, ta-DUM, ta-DUM, ta-DUM, ta-DUM.)

A sonnet has three quatrains (four-line stanzas) and ends with a couplet.

Its rhyme scheme is ABAB, CDCD, EFEF, GG.

Cinquain

A five-line, unrhymed poem with this pattern:

Line 1: One word that names the topic

Line 2: Two adjectives that define or describe the topic

Line 3: Three verbs ending in "ing" that express the topic's action

Line 4: Four words that express an effect or feeling the topic causes

Line 5: One word that is a synonym for the topic

An Example

> Mary
>
> Humble, sinless
>
> Obeying, helping, sorrowing
>
> She answers my prayers
>
> Mother

Diamante

A seven-line poem shaped like a diamond with this pattern:

Line 1: A noun

Line 2: Two adjectives that describe the noun

Line 3: Three verbs that end with "ing" and describe the noun

Line 4: Two nouns about the noun in line one and two about the noun in line seven

Line 5: Three verbs that end in "ing" and describes the noun in line seven

Line 6: Two adjectives that describe the noun in line seven

Line 7: A noun that is an antonym or synonym for the noun in line one

An Example

Jesus

Humble, merciful

Teaching, loving, healing

Kindness, compassion, courage, silence

Suffering, willing, sacrificing

Obedient, holy

Savior

Concrete

Single words or phrases forming a solid or outlined shape related to the topic

An Example

MARY   MARY

MARYMARYMARYMARY

MARYMARYMARYMARYMARY

MARYMARYMARYMARYMARYMA

MARYMARYMARYMARYMARY

YMARYMARYMARYMARYM

RYMARYMARYMARYMA

RYMARYMARYMAR

MARYMARY

MARY

- Write and illustrate a booklet that introduces a young child to Mary. To make a four-page accordion booklet, fold a long, rectangular piece of paper or tagboard in half and then fold back the sides to form a *W*. For eight pages, make two pieces folded as for four pages and then tape them together.

- Find out what people who loved Mary deeply said about her. For example, Saint John Vianney maintained, "The heart of Mary is so tender toward us that the love of all the mothers in the world put together are like a piece of ice in comparison to hers." Compile quotations about Mary like this one. Make a decorative plaque of one quotation about Mary. Paint on a wooden board or heavy cardboard. You might letter the quotation in calligraphy.

- Produce an issue of a Galilean newspaper focused on an event in Mary's life like the birth of Jesus or the wedding at Cana. Include a striking headline, a front-page article, other articles, an editorial, an ad, and a weather report.

- Write a eulogy for Mary that explains why she deserves praise and love.

- Compose a letter, postcard, or email that Mary might have written to Jesus, Anne, Elizabeth, Joseph, John the Baptist, or John the apostle. Or write a letter, postcard, or email that one of these people might have written to her.

- Write a meditation on something Mary experienced. Relate it to your own life.

- Tell the story of an episode in Mary's life from another person's point of view. Examples:

  – The Angel Gabriel gives an account of the annunciation.
  – A shepherd or one of the Magi tells about the nativity.
  – Anna recounts the Presentation.
  – A servant describes the miracle at Cana.
  – Mary Magdalene tells of Mary during the passion and death of her Son.

• Compose an entry for Mary in a book called *Who's Who in Israel.*

• Suppose texting was available in the first century. Write texts that Mary and Joseph might have sent to each other or that Mary and Jesus might have sent during his public ministry.

• Create a choral reading that is centered on Mary. Plan parts for individuals and groups to read. See **Appendix C** on page 77 for an example that you might carry out.

• Write an essay titled "When I Think of Mary."

Chapter 11

Churches Dedicated to God's Mother

The world was horrified in 2019 when fire severely damaged Notre Dame Cathedral in France. Of the countless basilicas, churches, chapels, and shrines that bear Mary's name, that cathedral is the most well-known. Victor Hugo's novel *The Hunchback of Notre-Dame* did much to popularize it. Notre Dame is one of around eighty cathedrals in Mary's honor built in France from 1140 to 1280. Every continent has at least one Marian church including Antarctica. The largest Christian church in the world is also named for her: the Basilica of Our Lady of Peace in Yamoussoukro, Côte d' Ivoire (Ivory Coast), in Africa. This basilica is larger than St. Peter's Basilica in Rome.

Activities

• Write a report on the Basilica of Saint Mary Major, which is the largest Marian church in Rome and one of the oldest churches there. It even has a feast day, August 5. Include why this church is also called Our Lady of the Snows and the lovely tradition carried out there on this feast.

• List churches in Rome that are named for Mary other than the Basilica of Saint Mary Major. Learn at least one special feature of three of them.

• Visit the website of the Basilica of the National Shrine of the Immaculate Conception in Washington, D.C., at https://www.nationalshrine.org/and take the virtual tour. Better still, visit this magnificent church in person. The Immaculate Conception is the patroness of the United States. The basilica houses more than eighty shrines dedicated to Mary under different titles and representing various countries.

• Learn the interesting history of Canada's national shrine to Mary, the basilica of Our Lady of the Cape in Quebec on the shore of the St. Lawrence River. Its construction involved a miraculous ice bridge.

• Learn about the Basilica of the Annunciation in Nazareth. Find out what its dome represents and what holy site is on its lower level. There are myriad pictures of Mary from different countries on the outside walls of the church's courtyard and the inside walls of the upper level. View them by going to https://www.biblewalks.com/Annunciation-Mosaics.

• Report on any or all the following notable churches names for Mary. Include their history, structure, and outstanding features.

  – Notre Dame Cathedral in Paris, France
  – The Cathedral of Our Lady of Chartres in Chartres, France, where a piece of Our Lady's veil is thought to be in a reliquary there
  – The Basilica of Our Lady of the Pillar in Zaragoza, Spain, which is the oldest church dedicated to Mary
  – Our Lady of La Leche in St. Augustine, Florida, which is the oldest Marian shrine in the United States

• Find out how many shrines to our Blessed Mother are in the United States. Choose one and report on it.

• List the churches in your diocese that are named for Our Blessed Mother. You might visit one of them and learn its history.

• Learn about a Marian shrine in your vicinity. Make a pilgrimage to it and pray for the world, people you love, and your needs.

• Note where your parish church has a side altar to Mary or an image of her inside or on the grounds. Discover its history.

• Compile a list of basilicas named for Mary in countries throughout the world. Write a report on one of them, perhaps the Basilica of Our Lady of Aparecida in Brazil, which is the largest Catholic country.

• Report on the Mary of Nazareth International Center in Nazareth, Israel, that opened in 2011.

• Find out the meaning of the Golden Rose, which popes have awarded to dozens of Marian basilicas and shrines. Which were the latest three to receive the Golden Rose?

• Look up Marian shrines where people who have prayed to Mary for healing left their wheelchairs, crutches, and other equipment for the sick and disabled after they were cured through her intercession.

• Learn about the two basilicas that are at Lourdes in France, which is one of the most popular places of pilgrimage. Write a report on them.

Things to Make

• Set up a Mary shrine on a table or shelf in your home. On a doily or lovely fabric, display an image of Mary along with flowers, a plant, or colorful leaves. Include a rosary.

• Create a Mary shrine in your yard. Place a statue of her there and add flowers and plants.

• Make a miniature shrine to Mary. Paint a tin box (like a breath mint tin) with acrylic paint. Trace the bottom on felt, fabric, or paper twice. Cut out the shapes and glue them inside the box. Place a picture or statue of Mary inside the box and glue it in place. Opposite it glue a paper with a prayer to Mary and a small artificial flower.

• Build a replica of a Marian basilica or church using sugar cubes, Legos, or other building blocks.

Chapter 12

Our Lady's Apparitions

One day during recess two little girls ran back into the school building and breathlessly told the principal, Sister Jonathan, "We saw Mary in the sky." Sister went outside and asked the supervising mother, "Did they really see Mary?" "Well, some clouds were shaped like her," the woman said. Turning to the girls, Sister asked, "What did you do when you saw Mary?" One girl replied, "First we said our First Communion prayers and then we said the Pledge of Allegiance."

The girls' vision was dubious. Nevertheless, in our modern era Mary has appeared on earth more often than in all other centuries combined. These apparitions show Mary's loving concern for us. Usually, she has a message, such as pray and do penance for peace and pray the Rosary. True apparitions never contradict a Church teaching.

The Church may judge an apparition worthy of belief and devotion, but because an apparition is considered a private revelation, no one is required to have faith in it. The places where our Blessed Mother appeared are pilgrimage sites, drawing thousands of people every year.

Apparitions that the Holy See of the Church has approved

Our Lady of Fatima, Portugal

Our Lady of Lourdes, France

Our Lady of Guadalupe, Mexico

Our Lady of the Miraculous Medal, France

Our Lady of LaSalette, France

Our Lady of Knock, Ireland

Apparitions approved by local bishops

Our Lady of the Good Event, Ecuador

Our Lady of Laus, France

Our Lady of Pontmain, France

Our Lady of Beauraing, Belgium

Our Lady of Banneux, Belgium

Our Lady of Akita, Japan

Our Lady of Good Help, Wisconsin, United States

Our Lady of Lezajsk, Poland

Our Lady of Kibeho, Rwanda, Africa

Other reported apparitions

Our Lady of Light, Zeitoun, Egypt

Our Lady in Medjugorje, Bosnia and Herzegovina

Our Lady of La Vang, Vietnam

Activities

• Learn about one of Mary's approved apparitions and write its story. Include why you think Mary appeared at that particular time and place.

• Interview someone who has visited a site where Mary appeared. Prepare your questions ahead of time. After the interview share with another person what you learned.

• Locate someone who has visited Lourdes, Fatima, the Basilica of Our Lady of Guadalupe in Mexico City, or another place where Mary appeared. Invite him or her to speak to your family or class and show photos or slides as well as memorabilia of the visit.

• Draw or paint a picture of one of our Blessed Mother's apparitions. Display it or keep it where it will remind you of Mary and prompt you to pray to her.

• Find and pray a prayer to Our Lady that addresses her by the title of one of her apparitions.

• Compose a prayer to Mary under the title of one of her apparitions.

• Look up the five prayers that Our Lady and the Angel of Peace gave the children of Fatima to pray. Make a prayer card of one or more of them.

• Read a biography of one of the following saints favored by an apparition of Mary and make a book report.

Saint Catherine of Siena	Saint Juan Diego	Saint Francisco
Saint Catherine Labouré	Saint Bernadette	Saint Jacinta

• Stage an interview with one of the people privileged to witness an apparition of Mary.

• Write a report on Mary's apparition to Saint James the Greater in 40 AD. This is thought to be Mary's first apparition after her assumption.

• Investigate one of the claims that an image of Mary has wept or moved. Sometimes this phenomenon is revealed as a fraud. Other times the cause remains a mystery.

• Imagine if our Blessed Mother appeared to you. What do you think she would say? What would you say to her?

• Locate a map of Mary's apparitions on the Internet.

• Find out about the book *Mystical City of God,* which is a record of a seventeenth-century nun's private revelations concerning Mary.

Chapter 13

Legends about Mary

Famous people tend to give rise to legends, usually to highlight one of their qualities. For example, who doesn't know the story of George Washington admitting that he chopped down a cherry tree? Love for Mary has prompted people to imagine stories about her as early as the apocryphal writings of the second century, such as the *Protoevangelium of James.* Marian legends flourished in the Middle Ages. Some of them are found in the popular Golden Legend, a collection of stories of saints originally compiled in the thirteenth century by the Dominican Jacobus de Varagine, Archbishop of Genoa, and expanded over the years.

Activities

• Investigate the following legends. Retell one or more of them in the form of a poem. See types of poems on pages 53–55.

Mary's miraculous birth

Mary's early life in the Temple

How Saint Joseph was designated as Mary's husband

The Virgin's Tree near Cairo, Egypt

The evangelist Saint Luke's icon of Mary

The black *M* on a tabby cat's forehead

Mary's house in Ephesus

Happenings related to Mary's assumption

The apostle Saint Thomas and Mary's belt

Mary's house in Loreto, Italy

Mary presenting the rosary to Saint Dominic

Our Lady's juggler

Origin of the Basilica of Saint Mary Major (Our Lady of the Snows)

• Research the following legends that associate flowers with Mary. Locate pictures of the flowers and create a booklet or a PowerPoint presentation on these legends.

Flower	Legend
Lilies	Eve and Mary
Lavender	Jesus' swaddling clothes
Columbines	Mary's shoes
Marigolds	Mary's purse
Lilies of the Valley	Mary's tears
Fuscia	Mary's earrings
Sea Pink (Sea Thrift)	The flight into Egypt
Violets	The annunciation, Christ's passion
Carnations	The death of Jesus

• Find out about legends connected with Marian statues:

Our Lady of Camarin, patron of Guam

Our Lady of Charity of El Cobre, patron of Cuba

Our Lady of Nazaré in Portugal

Our Lady of Clonfert, Ireland

• Create a child's book about one Marian legend.

• Portray a legend using any art medium, such as crayons, pastels, colored pencils, chalk, or paint.

Chapter 14

Miscellaneous Activities

The Internet is a rich source of material aimed to educate children about Mary. One site is www.teacherspayteachers.com. Worksheets and workbooks are time-honored tools for teachers. An example of a helpful book is *Enriching Faith: Lessons, Prayers and Activities on Mary* by Mary Kathleen Glavich, SND (Twenty-Third Publications), which contains thirty-two lessons for children.

Marian Words

See **Appendix G** on page 82 for Marian terms.

• Make a crossword puzzle. List terms related to Mary along with simple definitions. To design the puzzle, use an Internet site that generates crossword puzzles. Or work with pencil and paper and arrange the words so they go across and down and share some letters. Graph paper is recommended for this.

• Create a word search puzzle of words associated with Mary. Hide them vertically, horizontally, and diagonally. Use an Internet site that produces word searches. Or work out the puzzle with pencil and paper. Graph paper helps to keep the letters aligned.

• Design a word cloud of Marian terms. Vary the color, size, and font of the words. You might make your word cloud using a site on the Internet that creates word clouds.

- Make a dictionary of Marian terms. Set the words in alphabetical order and define them. Illustrate some of the entries in your booklet. Add a cover with a picture.

- Play Concentration. Make two identical sets of flashcards with Marian terms. Shuffle the sets together, place the cards facedown, and play the game: Players take turns flipping two cards. When the two cards match and the player correctly defines the term, he or she takes the cards and wins another turn. If the player is unsuccessful, the next player may define the term. The one who has collected the most cards at the end of the game wins.

The Meaning of Mary

- Ask three people what Mary means to them.

- Reflect on what our Blessed Mother means to you. Write a paragraph about it.

- Write an essay about what Mary meant to Jesus.

Mary in Film

- View a movie in which Mary is featured or plays an important role. Tell how the movie deepened your understanding and love of our Blessed Mother. Some possibilities are the following:

The Song of Bernadette
Fatima
Mary of Nazareth
Jesus of Nazareth
The Nativity Story
The Passion of the Christ
The Chosen

Mary in Social Media

• Create a podcast about our Blessed Mother.

• Design a website for Mary on paper. Create a homepage and at least two other pages.

• Set up a Pinterest page about Mary.

• Make a youTube or TikTok video on some aspect of Mary.

• Write a blog post about Our Lady if you or your parish has a website.

Board Game

On heavy paper or cardboard draw a path of squares that leads to a star. In each square write a word or phrase related to Mary. See **Appendix G** on page 82 for terms. Add art to the game if you wish. Provide a token like a penny or a button for each player.

Take turns rolling a die, moving the indicated number of spaces, and defining what the square landed on says. An incorrect or missing answer results in losing a turn or going back a square. The first person to reach the star wins.

Variation of the Board Game

• Prepare cards with Marian terms and place the deck face down. See **Appendix G** on page 82 for terms. After rolling the die, a player takes a card from the top of the deck and defines the term. If correct, the player may move the indicated number of spaces.

• Instead of terms, questions may be written on the cards. These might include the ones listed on the next page.

Possible Questions for a Board Game

Who was Mary's father?

Who was Mary's mother?

Who was Mary's husband?

In what town did Mary live?

Who occupied and oppressed Mary's country?

What does Immaculate Conception mean?

What angel appeared to Mary?

By whose power did Mary become pregnant?

What pregnant woman did Mary help?

Who was Mary's Son?

In what town did Mary give birth?

What ruler tried to kill Mary's baby?

What country did the Holy Family escape to?

Who foretold sorrow for Mary?

At what event did Mary prompt a miracle?

How long was young Jesus missing in Jerusalem?

In what building did Mary find her lost Son?

About how long did Jesus live with Mary?

Where was Mary when Jesus died?

To whom did Jesus entrust Mary at his death?

When did the Holy Spirit come again to Mary?

What feast celebrates Mary going to heaven body and soul?

What does Notre Dame mean?

What is the most common prayer to Mary?

How many sets of mysteries does a Rosary have?

What is one town where Mary appeared?

Under what title is Mary the patroness of the United States?

What relation is Mary to you?

Bingo

Write definitions of Marian terms from the list below on small flashcards. Prepare as many bingo cards as needed with twenty-five squares and the center one marked "Free." In each square write a Marian term. Use small pieces of paper or cardboard, buttons, or pennies as markers. To play, read a definition at random and players who have the matching word cover it. The one who has a vertical, horizontal, or diagonal row covered first wins. Options: The winner may also be the one to cover the four corners or the entire card.

Terms and Definitions

Theotokos	Greek word for Mother of God
Joachim	Mary's father
Anne	Mary's mother
Joseph	Mary's husband
Immaculate Conception	Mary's freedom from all sin
Annunciation	Angel Gabriel telling Mary that she would be God's mother
Holy Spirit	The Person through whose power Mary conceived Jesus
Nazareth	Mary's hometown
Israel	Country where Mary lived
Visitation	Mary's going to help pregnant Elizabeth
Bethlehem	Town where Mary gave birth to Jesus
Magi	Men from the East who gave gifts to Mary's child
Herod	Ruler who wanted to kill Jesus, the newborn king
Egypt	Country the Holy Family fled to
Simeon	The person who foretold sorrow for Mary at Jesus' Presentation
Temple	Where Mary found Jesus when he was missing
Cana wedding	Where Mary prompted Jesus to perform his first miracle
Pentecost	When the Holy Spirit came to Mary a second time
Calvary	Where Mary was when Jesus died
Saint John	Apostle to whom Jesus entrusted Mary

Assumption	Mary's going to heaven body and soul
Rosary	Prayer in which fifty-three Hail Marys are prayed on beads
Magnificat	Prayer Mary prayed when she visited Elizabeth
Fatima	Where Mary appeared to three shepherd children
Lourdes	Where Mary appeared to Bernadette and called herself the Immaculate Conception

Lapbook

Create a lapbook pertaining to Mary. Inside a file folder (or two glued together) attach items that contain information about our Blessed Mother or something related to her, such as the Rosary or sites dedicated to her. The items can be any of these:

– Mini-books

– Pockets of cards or slips of paper

– A wheel with facts written between the spokes

– A booklet in which pages fan out, held together by a ring or a round head fastener inserted in a hole punched in one corner

True or False

Decide whether the statements on **Appendix I** on page 85 are true or false. Then do research to find out if they are true. (Answers are on page 87.)

Appendix

A. Guided Meditation on the Wedding at Cana

Sit with feet flat on the floor and hands upturned. Breathe slowly a few times. Close your eyes.

You are a guest at the Cana wedding, a celebration that can last a week. This one has been going on for several days already. See the people filling the house and gathered outside. Hear the noise. Smell the food cooking. Some guests have had too much to drink. Instruments are playing, and a group of men are dancing together in a circle.

Inside the house Mary is speaking to two other women, overseeing the food they prepared. Nearby Jesus sits on a bench with four apostles. They are talking and laughing. You are seated a short distance away from them.

You see Mary glance over at the wine barrels. A servant is trying to fill a jug. Turning to the other servants, he shrugs and shakes his head. You would like your cup refilled, but it looks like the wine ran out. That is a social disaster. How humiliating for the newlyweds and their parents! You feel sorry for them.

Then you notice Mary quickly walking over to Jesus. She bends down and says in a low voice, "They have no wine." She trusts her Son to do something. You think that he and the apostles might leave the party to purchase more wine. But Jesus replies, "Woman, what concern is that to you and to me? My hour has not yet come." It doesn't sound like he's ready to begin his public ministry.

You expect Mary to be dismayed at her Son's words. She frowns, yet, she strides over to the servants and, pointing to Jesus, she orders, "Do whatever he tells you." Apparently, she's confident that Jesus can't resist her subtle plea for help. The servants are perplexed. They think, "What does that carpenter know about providing wine?" But Mary's calm demeanor and faith in her Son convinces them to do as she says.

Watch Jesus stand and stride over to six large stone jars. Hear him say to the servants, "Fill the jars with water." The servants are dumbfounded. Although they probably feel silly, they make trips to the well and pour water to the top of the jars—about 150 gallons, an enormous amount.

Jesus tells them to take some wine to the chief steward. See a servant dip a ladle into the jar and draw out what he expects will be water. As he pours the liquid into a cup, you see that it runs red. Look at the shock on the servant's face. You too are astounded.

The servants go to the chief steward, and one offers him the cup. You watch the steward take a drink. He smacks his lips and wipes them with the back of his hand. You hear him declare that usually the best wine is served first, but this excellent wine has been kept for last. You see Jesus wink at his mother. What you don't hear is Mary telling people that the wedding was saved because of her.

The jars held water for Jewish purification rituals. Someday Jesus would purify the world by sacrificing his blood.

Do you need something? Right now ask your heavenly mother for help.

B. Interviewing Saint Elizabeth

Today we are pleased to be speaking with Saint Elizabeth, the mother of John the Baptist.

Elizabeth, what was it like being pregnant after waiting so long?
Naturally Zechariah and I were thrilled. But I must admit, the first six months were difficult. I had to force myself to do my everyday tasks, especially with morning sickness. Lugging water from the well and pounding grain wore me out. But then Mary came and made my life easier.

Were you expecting Mary?
No, it was a total surprise. We didn't have cell phones or email like you do today. I never imagined that Mary would travel ninety miles to help me. The journey was a rough one: uphill on a rocky road under a hot sun. It was also dangerous because bandits often attacked the caravans. To think that Mary was pregnant when she made the trip is amazing. And when she traveled home three months later, she was even more pregnant. Mary made me feel precious and very loved.

Tell us about the day Mary arrived.
I was sweeping the floor. Suddenly I heard a young voice calling, "Elizabeth, it's Mary, your cousin from Nazareth." Just like that, the baby inside me jumped. Strangely, I immediately knew that Mary was pregnant with the Savior. I hugged her and exclaimed, "Blessed are you among women, and blessed is the fruit of your womb." I told Mary that she was blessed for believing that God would keep his promise to her. I was overcome by having the mother of the Lord come to me. What a privilege!

   Mary responded with a prayer praising God that you now call the Magnificat. She was so humble. She stated how God favored her who was a lowly servant. She mentioned how God helps the poor, and she acknowledged his mercy in keeping the promise he made to Abraham. Nowadays the Church prays Mary's prayer every evening in the Divine Office.

How did Mary assist you?
Mary helped me with daily chores like fetching water, preparing meals, doing the laundry, and shopping at the market. But what I really appreciated was her companionship. You know that my husband Zechariah was mute for not believing he would have a son. To communicate with others, he wrote on a board. But that didn't help me because I couldn't read. With Mary here, I had someone to talk with. She and I spent many hours sharing news about our relatives and discussing God's goodness to our people and our miraculous pregnancies. As we sewed baby clothes, we spoke about our hopes for our babies. Of course, back then we didn't know how our sons' lives would be entwined. My son John prepared the way for Mary's Son. It was a joy and an honor to be in the presence of Mary and the unborn Jesus for such a long time.

You are the patron saint of expectant mothers. How do you feel about that role?
I'm proud and happy to assist them. I like to help them like Mary helped me.

Thank you, Elizabeth, for your time. This was very informative.

C. Choral Reading Based on Luke 8:19-21

Parts: Narrator, Jesus, Voice 1, Voice 2, Voice 3

Narrator: Jesus was speaking to a large crowd.

Voice 1: Jesus, your mother and brothers are outside. They want to speak to you.

Jesus: My mother and my brothers are those who hear the word of God and do it.

Voice 2: What a putdown of his mother and brothers!

Voice 3: That wasn't a putdown but praise.

Narrator: Yes, Mary always heard and then kept God's word.

Side 1: God asked Mary to be his mother.

Side 2: Mary agreed at once.

All: Mary listened and said yes.

Side 1: God whispered in Mary's heart to go help pregnant Elizabeth.

Side 2: Mary hurried to Elizabeth, who lived in a town far away.

All: Mary listened and said yes.

Side 1: God had Mary travel to Bethlehem for a census.

Side 2: Mary left with Joseph although she was nine-months pregnant.

All: Mary listened and said yes.

Side 1: Through Joseph God told Mary to flee to Egypt with her baby.

Side 2: Mary packed and went immediately.

All: Mary listened and said yes.

Side 1: God nudged Mary to help when wine ran out at a wedding.

Side 2: Mary prompted Jesus to work his first miracle.

All: Mary listened and said yes.

Side 1: God told Mary on Calvary to care for John and us as her children.

Side 2: Mary loves and protects all of us as our heavenly mother.

All: Mary listened and said yes.

Narrator: Who more than Mary heard God's word and obeyed it?

D. Study Guide on *Lumen Gentium*, Chapter 8

52 If the Church is the Lord's body, who is its mother?

53 Because Mary was the mother of God the Son, what relation is she to Father and Holy Spirit?

Why did Mary need salvation?

For what two virtues in particular is Mary the Church's model?

54 What place does Mary hold in the Church?

55 What three things shed light on Mary's role in our salvation?

When was the salvation promised in the Old Testament fulfilled?

56 How did God respect Mary's free will? How did she respond?

What does it mean that Mary was "full of grace"?

How was Mary the opposite of Eve?

57 What four times after the Annunciation show Mary's union with Christ?

58 What did Jesus praise Mary for?

How did Mary show her union with Christ in his sacrifice?

59 When did the Holy Spirit come upon Mary a second time?

What privilege was Mary given after her life on earth?

What honor did Mary receive in heaven?

60 Why isn't Mary called our Mediator?

61 Why do we call Mary our mother?

62 How does Mary exercise her saving role today?

Who is the one Mediator who shares his role with Mary?

63 In what two ways does the Church resemble Mary?

After Mary's first-born, who else's birth and development does she care for?

64 How is the Church a mother like Mary? How is the Church a virgin like Mary?

65 How are we to be like Mary?

66 How does devotion to Mary affect our relationship with Christ?

67 What is true devotion to Mary?

68 How is Mary the image of the future Church?

69 What does Mary intercede for regarding the human family?

Answers are on page 86.

E. Mysteries of the Holy Rosary

The Joyful Mysteries

1. The Annunciation
   (Luke 1:26–28)

2. The Visitation
   (Luke 1:39–45)

3. The Birth of Jesus
   (Luke 2:1–20)

4. The Presentation in the Temple
   (Luke 2:22–38)

5. Finding of Jesus in the Temple
   (Luke 2:41–50)

The Luminous Mysteries

1. The Baptism of Jesus in the Jordan River
   (Matthew 3:17)

2. The Wedding at Cana
   (John 2:1–12)

3. The Proclamation of the Kingdom of God
   (Mark 1:15)

4. The Transfiguration
   (Luke 9:29)

5. The Institution of the Eucharist
   (Mark 14:22–26)

The Sorrowful Mysteries

1. The Agony in the Garden
   (Matthew 26:36–46)

2. The Scourging at the Pillar
   (Mark 15:6–16)

3. The Crowning with Thorns
   (Matthew 27:27–31)

4. The Carrying of the Cross
   (Mark 15:20–22)

5. The Crucifixion
   (Luke 23:33–46)

The Glorious Mysteries

1. The Resurrection
   (Matthew 28:1–10)

2. The Ascension of Our Lord
   (Luke 24:50–53)

3. The Descent of the Holy Spirit
   (Acts 2:1–13)

4. The Assumption of Our Lady into Heaven

5. The Coronation of the Blessed Virgin Mary

F. Directions for Making a Rose, Carnation, and Lily

A. Tissue Paper Rose or Carnation

Materials: White, pink, or red tissue paper; scissors

Method 1

1. Cut six pieces of tissue paper about 5" square.
2. Place the pieces on top of each other and accordion-fold them in ½" pleats.
3. Wrap the end of a pipe cleaner around the middle.
4. Cut the two ends of the pleated paper in a curve.
5. Spread out the two fans and turn up the ends.
6. Peel up each layer.
7. Fluff the ends so the flower looks like a rose.

Method 2

Use one soft facial tissue. Accordion-fold it long ways in ½" pleats. Fold it in half. Holding it closed, tie it in the middle with a twist tie, yarn, or ribbon. Cut through the folded end. Gently separate the layers.

B. A Lily

Materials: White paper, scissors, green chenille stem, yellow paper, green paper, tape, glue

1. Fold a 6" square of white paper in half diagonally.
2. Fold a side one-third of the way.
3. Fold the remaining third to cover that third.
4. Draw a long petal on the front from side to side.
5. Cut out the petal through the six layers of paper.
6. Open the flower and tape the two ends together.
7. Pull each petal between your thumb and a scissor blade to curl it outward.
8. Insert a green chenille stick inside the lily for the stem.

---

9. Cut three stamens from yellow paper and glue them inside the lily.

10. Cut leaves from green paper and attach them to the stem.

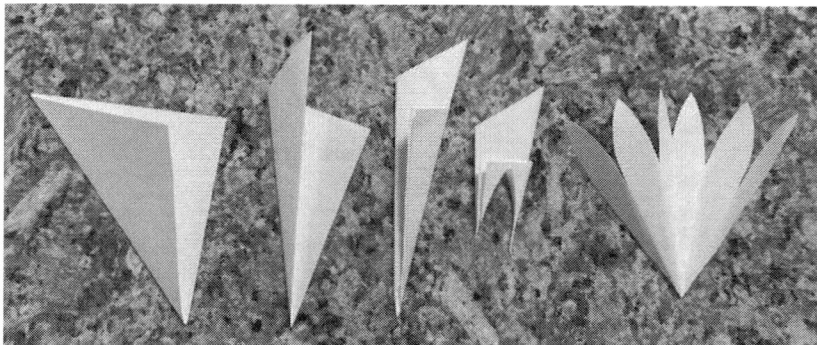

G. Marian Terms

Anne	Joseph
Annunciation	Lourdes
Assumption	Magi
Bethlehem	Mother
Calvary	Nazareth
Cana wedding	Pentecost
Egypt	Queen
Elizabeth	Rosary
Fatima	Saint John
Gabriel	Scapular
Herod	Simeon
Holy Spirit	Theotokos
Immaculate Conception	Virgin
Jesus	Visitation
Joachim	

H. Garden of Virtues Prayer Service

A Marian hymn followed by the Rosary's opening prayers

Leader: Saint John of the Cross said, "Each of us is called to cultivate an inner garden in which the Divine Word may grow and flourish." Let us pray today for the grace to plant Mary's virtues in the garden of our soul.

Side 1: A sunflower, which always faces the sun, symbolizes faith. People of faith always trustingly look to God.

Side 2: Mary was not afraid to say yes to whatever God asked. She believed in God's love for her.

All: Mary, may we always stay true to God and his will for us.

~ Decade of the Rosary: *The Annunciation*

Side 1: A violet, a gentle, delicate flower, stands for humility. Humble people are unassuming and modest. They don't talk about themselves or brag.

Side 2: When Mary visited Elizabeth, she foretold that all ages would call her blessed. But she was not conceited. She realized that her holiness was a gift from God.

All: Mary, pray that we see ourselves as we truly are, as God sees us.

~ Decade of the Rosary: *The Visitation*

Side 1: A daisy, with its simple, white petals, stands for purity. Pure people are innocent of sin.

Side 2: Mary was untouched by sin from the first moment of her existence.

All: Mary, help us to avoid people, places, and things that may lead us to sin.

~ Decade of the Rosary: *The Nativity*

Side 1: Edelweiss, which grows in the mountains, stands for courage in the face of uncertainty. Courageous people dare to take risks in doing what is right.

Side 2: Mary showed holy boldness in agreeing to be the Mother of God, in traveling to help Elizabeth, and in accompanying Jesus to Calvary.

All: Mary, help me be courageous in living out my faith.

~ Decade of the Rosary: *The Presentation*

Side 1: A rose, known for its beauty and fragrance, symbolizes love.

Side 2: Mary showed love for God by devoting her whole life to him. She showed love for others when, although pregnant, she made the long journey to help Elizabeth and when she prompted Jesus to provide wine at the wedding. Mary also showed love for us by taking on the role of our heavenly Mother.

All: Mary, may my heart be filled with love for God and for other people, especially those who are in need.

~ Decade of the Rosary: *The Finding of Jesus in the Temple*

* * *

All: Hail, Holy Queen, Mother of Mercy,
   our life, our sweetness, and our hope.
To you do we cry, poor banished children of Eve.
To you do we send up our sighs, mourning and weeping in this valley of tears.
Turn then, most gracious advocate, your eyes of mercy toward us,
   and after this our exile, show unto us the blessed fruit of your womb, Jesus.

O clement, O loving, O sweet Virgin Mary!
Pray for us, O holy Mother of God.
That we may be made worthy of the promises of Christ.

I. True or False Statements

1. The Quran, the Muslim holy book, has more verses about Mary than the Catholic Bible.

2. The state of Maryland was named for the Blessed Virgin.

3. Martin Luther prayed the Rosary every day until he died.

4. The Marianum, a pontifical institute in Rome, has more than 85,000 books on Mary.

5. The Church teaches that Mary died.

6. Mary's Assumption was not declared a dogma until 1950.

7. Church bells were rung three times a day, reminding people to pray the Angelus.

8. "O Sanctissima" is thought to have originated with Sicilian fishermen asking Mary's protection during the night.

9. The largest Christian church in the world is the Basilica of Our Lady of Peace in Asia.

10. After an assassin's attack on May 13, the Feast of Our Lady of Fatima, Pope John Paul II had one of the bullets that struck him placed in Our Lady's crown in Fatima.

11. The names for Mary's parents and the story of her Presentation in the temple are found in the Gospel of Luke.

12. At first people prayed fifty Our Fathers on beads called paternosters. Supposedly Lady Godiva bequeathed hers to a monastery.

13. The patron of the United States is Mary's husband, St. Joseph.

14. The largest statue of Mary in the United States is the 90-foot Our Lady of the Rockies.

15. Ladybugs are named for Mary.

52 Mary, the mother of Jesus

53 Mary is the daughter of the Father and the temple of the Holy Spirit.

Mary is a human being.

Mary is our model of faith and charity.

54 Mary is the highest after Christ and very close to us.

55 The Old and New Testaments and tradition

When the Son of God took a human nature from Mary

56 God awaited Mary's consent.

Mary said, "Be it done to me according to thy word."

Mary was entirely holy and free from sin.

Eve disobeyed and caused death; Mary obeyed and brought forth Life.

57 The visitation, the nativity, the presentation, the finding of Jesus in the temple

58 Mary heard and kept the Word of God.

Mary stood at the cross.

59 At Pentecost

Mary went to heaven body and soul.

The Lord made Mary Queen of all.

60 Jesus Christ is our one and only Mediator.

61 Mary cooperated in restoring supernatural life to souls.

62 Mary intercedes for us.

Jesus is the one Mediator.

63 The Church is mother and virgin.

Mary cares for the faithful, the brothers and sisters of Jesus.

64 The Church is mother by accepting God's words in faith and bringing others to immortal life.

The Church is virgin by being faithful to God.

65 We are to strive to increase in holiness by conquering sin and doing God's will.

66 Devotion to Mary make Jesus known, loved, glorified, and obeyed.

67 True devotion is not exaggerated, reduced, or emotional but comes from faith.

68 Mary's bodily and spiritual glory is what awaits the Church in the next world

69 Mary prays that all people be gathered in peace and harmony into the one People of God.

Answers to True or False Statements in Appendix I

1. True.

2. False. It is named after Queen Mary, wife of Charles I, King of England, Scotland, and Ireland.

3. True

4. True

5. False. The Church has no official teaching on Mary's death.

6. True

7. True

8. True

9. False. This basilica is in the Ivory Coast, Africa.

10. True

11. False. They are in the apocryphal Gospel the *Protoevangelium of Saint James*.

12. True

13. False. The Immaculate Conception is the patroness.

14. True

15. True

Other Books by Sister Mary Kathleen

Enriching Faith: Lessons, Prayers and Activities on Mary

The Catholic Companion to Mary

Heart to Heart with Mary: A Yearly Devotional

The Holy Spirit: Font of Love, Life, and Power

Jumbo Book of Art Ideas for Teachers and Parents

A Love Affair with God: Twelve Traits

Saint Teresa of Kolkata: Missionary of Charity

Praying on Empty: A Guide to Rediscovering Your Prayerful Self

I Am Going . . . : Reflections on the Last Words of the Saints

The Fisherman's Wife: The Gospel According to St. Peter's Spouse

Book of Ruth: A Tale of Great Loves

The Walking Love of God: St. Julie Billiart

Praying with Scripture: The Bible: You've Got Mail

The Catholic Companion to Jesus

The Catholic Companion to the Psalms

The Heartbeat of Faith: 59 Poems, Fingerplays, and Prayers

Why Is Jesus in the Microwave? Funny Stories from Catholic Classrooms

Voices: God Speaking in Creation

Totally Catholic! A Catechism for Kids and Their Parents and Teachers

Kindly write a review of this book on Amazon's website.
The author would appreciate it.

Made in the USA
Las Vegas, NV
10 March 2025